Heart & Soul of the Japanese

Yamakuse Yoji
Michael A. Cooney = translator

日本人のこころ

山久瀬 洋二
マイケル・クーニー＝訳

Furigana JAPAN

日本人のこころ
Heart & Soul of the Japanese

© 2011 Yoji Yamakuse
© 2017 IBC Publishing, Inc.

Published by IBC Publishing, Inc.
Ryoshu Kagurazaka Bldg. 9F, 29-3 Nakazato-cho
Shinjuku-ku, Tokyo 162-0804, Japan

www.ibcpub.co.jp

All rights reserved. No part of this book may be reproduced in
any form without written permission from the publisher.

First edition 2017

ISBN978-4-7946-0511-5

Printed in Japan

About *Furigana JAPAN*

Reading Sets You Free

The difficulty of reading Japanese is perhaps the greatest obstacle to the speedy mastery of the language. A highly motivated English speaker who wants to make rapid progress in a major European language such as Spanish, French or German need only acquire a grasp of the grammar and a smattering of vocabulary to become able to at least attempt to read a book. Thanks to a common alphabet, they can instantly identify every word on the page, locate them in a dictionary, and figure out—more or less—what is going on.

With Japanese, however, *kanji* ideograms make it infinitely harder to make the jump from reading with guidance from a teacher to reading freely by oneself. The chasm dividing the short example sentences of textbooks from the more intellectually rewarding world of real-world books and articles can appear unbridgeable. Japanese—to borrow Nassim Taleb's phrase—is an "Extremistan" language. *Either* you master two thousand *kanji* characters with their various readings to achieve breakthrough reading proficiency and the capacity for self-study *or* you fail to memorize enough *kanji*, your morale collapses, and you retire, tired of floating in a limbo of semi-literacy. At a certain point, Japanese is all or nothing, win or lose, put up or shut up.

The benefits of staying the course and acquiring the ability to read independently are, of course, enormous.

Firstly, acquiring the ability to study by yourself without needing a teacher increases the absolute number of hours that you can study from "classroom time only" to "as long as you want." If there is any truth to the theories about 10,000 hours of practise being needed to master any skill, then clearly the ability to log more hours of Japanese self-study has got to be a major competitive advantage.

Secondly, exposure to longer texts means that your Japanese

3

input rises in simple quantitative terms. More Japanese *going into* your head means that, necessarily, more Japanese *stays in* your head! As well as retaining more words and idioms, you will also start to develop greater mental stamina. You will get accustomed to digesting Japanese in real-life "adult" portions rather than the child-sized portions you were used to in the classroom.

Thirdly, reading will help you develop tolerance for complexity as you start using context to help you figure things out for yourself. When reading a book, the process goes something like this: You read a sentence; should you fail to understand it first time, you read it again. Should it still not make sense to you, you can go onto the next sentence and use the meaning of that one to "reverse-engineer" the meaning of its predecessor, and so on. By doing this, you will become self-reliant, pragmatic and—this is significant—able to put up with gaps in your understanding without panicking, because you know they are only temporary. You will morph into a woodsman of language, able to live off the land, however it may be.

That is the main purpose of *Furigana JAPAN*: to propel you across the chasm that separates those who read Japanese from those who cannot.

Furigana the Equalizer

Bilingual books have been popular in Japan since the 1990s. Over time, they have grown more sophisticated, adding features like comprehensive page-by-page glossaries, illustrations and online audio. What makes the *Furigana JAPAN* series—a relative latecomer to the scene—special?

The clue is in the name. This is the first ever series of bilingual books to include *furigana* superscript above every single *kanji* word in the text. Commonly used in children's books in Japan, *furigana* is a tried-and-tested, non-intrusive and efficient way to learn to read *kanji* ideograms. By enabling you to decipher every word immediately, *furigana* helps you grasp the meaning of whole passages faster without needing to get bogged down in fruitless and demoralizing searches for the pronunciation of individual words.

By providing you with the pronunciation, *furigana* also enables you to commit new words to memory right away (since we remember more by sound than by appearance), as well as giving you the wherewithal to look them up, should you want to go beyond the single usage example on the facing English page. *Furigana JAPAN* provides a mini-glossary at the foot of each page to help you identify and commit to memory the most important words and phrases.

Raw Materials for Conversation

So much for *furigana*—now for the "Japan" part of the name. The books in this series are all about Japan, from its customs, traditions and cuisine to its history, politics and economy. Providing essential insights into what makes the Japanese and their society tick, every book can help you as you transition from ignorant outsider to informed insider. The information the books contain gives you a treasure trove of raw materials you can use in conversations with Japanese people. Whether you want to amaze your interlocutors with your knowledge of Japanese religion, impress your work colleagues with your mastery of party-seating etiquette and correct bowing angles, or enjoy a heated discussion of the relative merits of arranged marriages versus love marriages, *Furigana JAPAN* is very much the gift that keeps on giving.

We are confident that this series will help everyone—from students to businesspeople and diplomats to tourists—start reading Japanese painlessly while also learning about Japanese culture. Enjoy!

Tom Christian
Editor-in-Chief
Furigana JAPAN Series

まえがき

日本の伝統的な価値観や思想といった「日本の心」を、欧米の人にいかに伝えるかという試みは、今まで何度となく繰り返されてきました。

古くは、新渡戸稲造の『武士道』や岡倉天心の『茶の本』にはじまり、戦後になってからは数えきれない関連書籍が出版されました。

そして、日本人の価値観についての著書としては、第二次世界大戦末期から戦後にかけて執筆された、アメリカ人の著者、ルース・ベネディクトの『菊と刀』がよく知られています。

これらの書籍に共通して取り上げられた「恩」や「義理」といった日本人の心の原点ともいえる価値は、一体どこからきて、今の日本ではどのように捉えられているのでしょうか。本書はその壮大なテーマに挑み、日本を代表する「日本人の心」を70選びまとめてみました。

また、今となっては古くさえ思える価値観の中にも、実は現代人の心の奥にちゃんと残り、形を変えて影響を与えているものがあります。あるいは、その価値観によって行動するが故に、海外の人との誤解が生まれそうなものなど、様々な視点からそれらを見つめてみました。

本書をご一読いただき、そして、自らの経験や体験を取り込んで、自分の言葉としていかに日本の心を伝えてゆくか、読者の方々に御一考いただければ幸いです。

山久瀬　洋二

Preface

Many people, in days gone by, have made innumerable attempts to enlighten the West about traditional Japanese thought and the country's system of values—that is, "the heart of Japan."

This effort started in the distant past with Inazo Nitobe's *Bushido: The Soul of Japan* and Tenshin Okakura's *Book of Tea*, and in the postwar period it continued with the publication of countless similar works.

And not to be forgotten is the well-known book by Ruth Benedict that was begun near the end of World War II and finished after the war—*The Chrysanthemum and the Sword*.

One thing that is shared by all these works is their emphasis on "obligation" and "duty" as central principles in the Japanese value system. Where did these values come from, and what place do they have in modern Japanese life? In an attempt to answer this daunting question, I examine in this book 70 aspects of the "Japanese heart."

Some of the values that might appear antiquated today are still lingering in the further recesses of the minds of modern Japanese, having changed their forms but retained their influence. Other values may generate behavior that leads to potential misunderstandings with non-Japanese people. In such ways as this, I have examined Japanese values from various perspectives, hoping to pin them down.

I will be immensely pleased if, by reading this book, you can grasp the connections between the various elements of the Japanese heart, relating them to your own experiences and history.

Yamakuse Yoji

「日本人の心」を読み解くにあたって

　「日本人の心」を構成する価値観の基本の位置に、最初に紹介する「和」をおき、そこから様々な価値がどう関連してゆくかを考えれば、下図のようになります。

　どのような文化でも、その中にある価値が摩擦を起こすことなく共存でき、実践できたとき、人は安心感をもつものです。「和」こそは、日本人にとっての安心感で、それを抱くために、人は本書で紹介する様々な価値や行動規範、そして道徳を実践しようとするのです。

　そして、日本の場合、トータルな価値の和が整えられている人が「徳」のある人で、そうした人は、日本人の「美」意識も体得できるというわけです。

　この図を参照しながら、本文を読んでゆけば、それぞれの価値がどのように結びついているかが理解できるはずです。

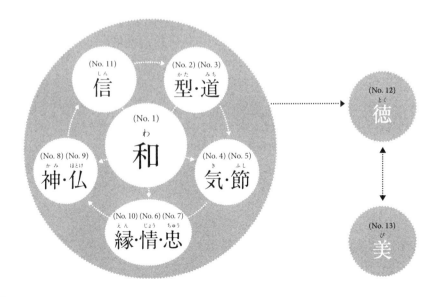

On Reading the "Japanese Heart"

If we take harmony (*wa*), the first value to be dealt with in this book, as the principal value in the Japanese system and position it in the center, showing its relative relation to other values, then we get the illustration seen below.

No matter what the culture, if its constituent values can coexist and function together without friction, the people inhabiting that culture feel a sense of tranquility.

Harmony represents tranquility for the Japanese, and in order to achieve it, a Japanese will adhere to the various values, norms, and moral precepts described in this book.

In Japan, a person who embodies the totality of values inherent in harmony is a person of virtue and can also embody the Japanese sense of beauty.

If you have reference to this illustration while reading the book, you will be able to understand how each value is linked to the others.

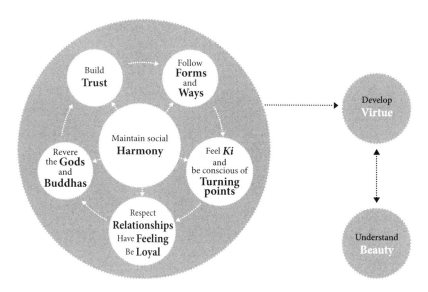

目次 Contents

まえがき
Preface..6

「日本人の心」を読み解くにあたって
On Reading the Japanese Heart................................8

1 和 Harmony..15

和 *Harmony*...16

謙譲と謙遜 *Modesty*.......................................18

遠慮 *Reserve*..20

場 *Place, Situation*...22

根回し *Lobbying*..24

2 型 Form, Way of Doing Things.....................29

型 *Form*...30

修練 *Discipline*..34

匠 *Craft*..36

3 道 Way..39

道 *Way, Road*..40

道理 *Reason*...42

武士道 *The Way of the Warrior*......................44

業 *Training*..48

求道 *Seeking the Truth*..................................50

4 　気　Energy 55

気　*Energy* 56
運気　*Fate* 60
殺気　*Sensing Danger* 62
空気　*Air, Atmosphere* 64

5 　節　Period 67

節と節目　*Period* 68
有終　*Beautiful Ending* 72
節度　*Restraint* 74
けじめ　*Marking a Break* 78

6 　情　Feelings 81

情　*Feelings* 82
人情　*Personal Feelings* 84
義理　*Obligation, Duty* 88
恩　*Social Debt* 92
内と外　*Inside and Outside, Social Circle* 96
本音と建前　*True Feelings and Facade* 100

7 　忠　Loyalty 103

忠　*Loyalty* 104
上下　*Hierarchy* 106
奉公　*Service* 108
忠義　*Loyalty* 110

孝 *Filial Piety* 112

しがらみ *Barriers* 114

8 神 The Gods 117

神 *The Gods* 118

禊 *Purification* 122

穢れ *Defilement* 124

願 *Request* 126

大和魂 *Japanese Spirit* 128

9 仏 Buddhism 131

仏 *Buddhism* 132

自力と他力 *Self-power and Other-power* 134

あの世 *The Other World* 136

ものの哀れ *Pathos* 140

無常 *Transience* 142

悟り *Enlightenment* 144

禅 *Zen* 146

煩悩 *Worldly Desires* 148

空 *Emptiness* 150

無 *Nothingness* 152

10 縁 Relationships 155

縁 *Relationships* 156

輪廻 *Reincarnation* 158

因果 *Cause and Effect* 160

11 信 Trust 163

信 *Trust* 164

仁 *Benevolence* 166

仁義 *Moral Code* 170

12 徳 Virtue 173

徳 *Virtue* 174

名 *Name* 176

恥 *Shame* 178

面目 *Face* 180

分 *Role* 182

阿吽の呼吸 *Intuitive Communication* 184

諦観 *Resignation* 186

13 美 Beauty 189

美 *Beauty* 190

わび *The Beauty of the Simple* 192

さび *The Beauty of the Decaying* 194

艶 *Refinement* 196

雅 *Elegance* 198

色 *Erotic* 200

粋 *Chic* 202

幽玄 *Profound Tranquility* 204

風流 *Cultured* 206

1

和
わ
Harmony

和

「和」とは、そのまま訳せばharmonyです。

「和」はまた日本を表す別の表現でもあります。たとえば日本食のことを、日本人は和食ともいいます。日本の**伝統的な**服は和服と呼びます。

「和」とは、人と人とがいかに**心地よく**、共に過ごし、働くかということを表す**価値観**です。

日本は伝統的に、限られた土地を皆で耕作して、生活をしてきた農耕社会によって**成り立って**きました。この社会を成り立たせるためには、村人が自らのニーズよりも、村全体のニーズを考え、他の人々と行動を共にして稲を植え、収穫を**しなければなりません**。

したがって、日本には、個人の力量や行動を価値基準の中心におく狩猟社会や移民社会とは異なる、常に相手との絆を気遣い、グループで行動すること**をよしとする**価値基準が育まれました。それが「和」という**価値観**なのです。

日本人にとって「和」は、日本人の心の中に**培われた**全ての価値観の要となる考え方なのです。

16 | 和わ

Harmony

While the Chinese character for *wa* directly means "harmony," it is also used to mean "Japan." For example, Japanese cuisine is known as *wa-shoku* and Japanese clothing is known as *wa-fuku*.

"Harmony" is a basic value defined as the ability of people to cooperate pleasantly and work together well.

Japan is a country whose traditions developed out of an agricultural society where people were forced to work closely together on a limited amount of land. In order to maintain this type of society, the needs of the village were more important than the needs of the individual, as all labored together to plant the rice and harvest the crop.

Therefore, as opposed to hunter- or immigrant-based societies, where a high value is placed on the power or actions of the individual, a society developed in Japan where the value is placed on understanding those with whom one must interact and on taking action in groups. That is the definition of *wa*.

Wa is at the heart of what has been necessary to nurture everything in the Japanese value system.

□ そのまま directly
□ 伝統的な traditional
□ 心地よく pleasantly
□ 価値観 value
□ 成り立つ maintain

□ 〜なければならない must
□ したがって therefore
□ 〜をよしとする the value is placed on 〜ing
□ 培う to nurture
□ 要 heart

謙譲と謙遜

「和」をもって人とつき合うとき、お互いが自我を出しあって、自らの能力を強調し合ってばかりいると、物事がうまく進みません。日本人はこういうとき、むしろ自らの能力を抑え、相手に敬意を払いながら、相手との関係を構築します。この自分をへりくだり、相手に対して敢えて自らの能力を表明しない考え方を「謙譲」といいます。

相手も、「私は何もわかりませんが」といわれると、それを言葉通りには受け止めません。逆に日本では、能力のある人ほど、自分のことを低く表現することがよいこととされているために、このようにいう相手は、**かえって尊敬**されるのです。

この「謙譲」の価値観を実際の**言葉遣い**で表すとき、人は「謙遜する」という表現を使います。この言葉こそは、日本人の極めて大切な行動原理となっているのです。

「謙遜する」という行為は、時には家族や会社の同僚を紹介するときに使われます。自分の子供を紹介するとき、「何もできない愚息ですが」などといって紹介する習わしがそれにあたります。

自らの能力を率直に表現することをよしとする文化背景からきた外国の人には、この日本人の行動原理がわからず、**戸惑いを覚える**ことがよくあるようです。

「実るほど**頭を垂れる稲穂**かな」という日本人の好きな言葉があります。また、「**能ある鷹は爪を隠す**」という言葉も有名です。これは全て「謙遜」することの美学を伝える言葉なのです。

18 ┃ 和ゎ

Modesty

When using *wa* as the basis for a relationship, things will not go smoothly if both parties egotistically emphasize their own capabilities. A Japanese person would in fact downplay his own capabilities while paying respect to the other person and build the relationship in that way. This concept of putting oneself below another and not presuming to show one's capabilities is called *kenjō*.

One cannot take the words at their face value when one is told: "I don't know anything." In Japan, the greater the capabilities of a person, the more modestly he will state those capabilities, and thus in fact such persons are more respected.

When stating the value of *kenjō* in a sentence, it is common to use the word *kenson*, as in *kenson suru* ("being modest"). *Kenson* is a very important word in Japanese, reflecting the basic principles of the culture.

The concept of *kenson* is often used when introducing a member of one's family or company. This is evident in the phrase "good-for-nothing son" when introducing one's son, for example.

It seems that much confusion is created by the Japanese using this principle of *kenson* with non-Japanese whose cultures value straight forward expression of one's capabilities.

"The heavier the stock of rice, the more its head is lowered" is an expression well liked by the Japanese. "A wise hawk hides its talons" is another well-known phrase. These all convey the beauty of the concept of *kenson*.

□ 和をもって using *wa* as the basis
□ 自我を出し egotistically
□ 敬意を払う to pay respect
□ へりくだる to put oneself below another
□ かえって (but) in fact

□ 言葉遣い expression
□ あたる to correspond
□ 率直に表現する straight forward expression
□ 戸惑いを覚える to get bewildered
□ 頭を垂れる to lower one's head

Harmony | 19

遠慮

「和」を保つために最も考えなければならないことは、相手のことを慮る気持ちです。相手の状況を考えて、自らの行動を抑制し、相手に迷惑にならないようにすることを「遠慮」といいます。

遠慮の「遠」は遠くを、そして「慮」は思いめぐらすことを意味します。つまり、つねに先に思いを巡らして、相手に対応する心がけが「遠慮」なのです。躊躇という言葉がありますが、これは何かをすれば状況が悪くなるのではと恐れて行動を抑制することを意味します。

それに対して「遠慮」は、むしろそうなる前にしっかりと相手のことを考えて、相手のために行動を差し控える未来に向けた心構えなのです。相手に聞くまでもなく、自らが相手の気持ちを判断して、たとえば「今この話をすると相手が不快だろうから、遠慮して別の機会にしておこう」などと考えるのです。

言葉をもって明快に自らのニーズを伝え、それに対応することをよしとする欧米の文化からしてみると、この「遠慮」という考え方を理解することは困難です。躊躇がさらに未来の行動へと延長すると思えばわかりやすいのかもしれませんが、国際舞台では、日本人はついつい「遠慮」をしすぎて、自らの意思を伝えるチャンスを失っているようでもありますね。

現在では、「遠慮」という言葉をそのまま、「禁止する」と同じ意味に使うことも多々あります。「タバコはご遠慮ください」といえば、禁煙を丁寧に相手に伝えることになるのです。

Reserve

To maintain *wa*, it is always very important to give careful consideration to the feelings of the person with whom one is dealing. Understanding the circumstances of the other person and controlling one's actions so as not to cause trouble to that person is called *enryo*.

The first Chinese character of *en* in *enryo* means "distant," while the second character of *ryo* means "to think about." In other words, always thinking ahead about how to deal with other people is *enryo*. The word *chūcho* means "to hesitate," and is used in describing a situation in which a person refrains from taking action due to fear that circumstances will worsen.

Enryo, on the other hand, means thinking ahead before a situation develops, taking fully into account the other person, and then refraining from action based on those circumstances.

Without asking, one should be able to judge the feelings of the other person and decide if *enryo* is necessary. For example, "If I bring this up now, I'll make the other person feel uncomfortable, so I'll wait until another time."

In a culture where people are expected to speak up and make their needs known, with action being taken based on those requests, it is difficult for Westerners to understand the concept of *enryo*. Westerners, they may be able to understand *enryo* as an extension of *chūcho*, or hesitation, but too often the Japanese lose the chance to speak out on issues on the international stage due to their tendency towards *enryo*.

Nowadays the word *enryo* is also often used to mean "prohibited." For example, *tabako wa go-enryo kudasai* is a polite way of telling people that smoking is prohibited.

☐ 慮る to give careful consideration
☐ ～にならないようにする so as not to cause
☐ 思いめぐらす to think about
☐ つまり In other words
☐ 心がけ thinking ahead

☐ それに対して on the other hand
☐ 差し控える to refrain from action
☐ 心構え thinking ahead
☐ ついつい too often

Harmony

場

「遠慮」という考え方を理解するために必要なのがこの「場」という概念です。「場」とはいうまでもなく場所を意味します。そして、どういう場所でどのような行動をするかということを暗に示したのが「場」という概念なのです。

この「場」という考え方は、欧米でもあるようです。たとえば、結婚式を例にとれば、正式に教会や神社で行う儀式と、その後で披露宴などのパーティーでの人々の行動は自ずと違ってきます。儀式の間はしきたりに従い、パーティーでは比較的自由に人々は交流します。**すなわち、「場」が違えば、それぞれ「場」に合った行動が求められるのです。**

日本では日本人の価値観や行動様式に従って、外国人には見えない「場」がたくさんあります。お客さんとの正式な打合せの「場」での態度や、上司の前という「場」でのものの言い方、またはくだけたお酒の席という「場」での発言など、「場」によって人の行動が細かく変わり、時にはその「場」の状況によって、人は行動を差し控え「遠慮」することもあるのです。

「場をわきまえる」という言葉がありますが、「場」の状況をしっかりと理解して、その時に何をすべきかを的確に判断することが、日本での礼儀作法の第一歩といえます。

微妙な「場」の違いに気付かない外国人は、**時には不作法をしてし**まうかもしれません。

Place, Situation

To understand the thinking behind *enryo*, the concept of *ba* is necessary. It goes without saying that *ba* refers to "place." What actions happen in what place is implicit within the concept of *ba*.

The idea of *ba*, "place," also exists in the West. For example, in the case of a wedding, the actions of people at the ceremony at the church or temple are naturally different from people's actions at the reception afterwards. At the ceremony there are strict practices to follow, while at the reception people interact in a relatively free manner. In other words, because the *ba*, "place," is different, different actions are required.

There are many *ba* in Japan where the basic values and actions of the Japanese are employed, and these *ba* may be difficult for the non-Japanese to understand. The words and actions of a formal meeting with a customer will differ from those in a meeting with one's boss, and will differ again in the informal atmosphere of a night out on the town. At times, the concept of *enryo* will be necessary within the context of a particular *ba*.

The expression *ba wo wakimaeru* means to clearly understand the circumstances of a particular *ba*. Being able to make proper judgments about what to do based on the particular time and place is a first step towards truly grasping the basics of Japanese etiquette.

Sometimes a non-Japanese, not understanding the subtleties of a particular *ba*, will commit a faux pas.

□ 〜はいうまでもなく It goes without saying that 〜
□ 暗に示す implicit
□ 例にとれば in the case of
□ 自ずと naturally
□ すなわち in other words

□ くだけた informal
□ わきまえる to clearly understand the circumstances
□ 何をすべきか about what to do
□ 時には sometimes

Harmony | 23

根回し

　人との「和」を保ち、賢く自らの意見を 公 で発表するために、日本人は適切な「場」を選び、「間」も考慮して慎重に人とその情報を 共有してゆきます。こうした日本人の行動様式の典型が「根回し」という意思伝達方法なのです。

　会議の「場」でいきなりプレゼンテーションを行うと、場合によっては上司や関係者と意見の対立を生むリスクがあります。それを避けるために、関係する人に会議の前にその情報を伝えたり、必要に応じて提案内容を 調整することを「根回し」というのです。

　「根回し」が首尾よく行われていれば、会議の「場」で紛糾することなく、案件が承認されるわけです。

　非公式で「根回し」をするのはよくあることです。時には夕食やゴルフなどの会合といった職場から離れたプライベートな「場」で行われることもあります。

　そして、「根回し」をしっかりと繰り返すことで、人と公然と対立せずに、情報が共有され、企画やアイデアに関する情報が共有されるのです。

　根回しのそもそもの意味は、木を移植するときに、根を掘り起こし、それを傷つかないように丸く包んで移動させる方法のことです。

　すなわち、木を移植するときと同じように、関係者一人一人と話すことによって、人の輪をつくり、それを包み込んで公式の場に持ち込む方法が「根回し」なのです。

Lobbying

In order to preserve harmony (*wa*) when going "on the record" with an opinion, the Japanese will cautiously share information with others after careful consideration of the place and the timing. A very typical Japanese form of communicating one's will in this situation would be *nemawashi* (literally "loosening the roots").

If one presents a proposal for the first time right at a meeting, there is a risk that one's superiors or others affected by the proposal will have a different opinion. Avoiding this risk by consulting prior to the meeting with key persons and adjusting one's proposal as necessary is called *nemawashi* ("lobbying").

If one has done a thorough job of *nemawashi*, there should be little opposition at the meeting and the proposal should be approved.

It is common for *nemawashi* to take place outside the office, perhaps over dinner or while playing golf or at some other private setting (*ba*).

Through the repetition of *nemawashi*, there will naturally be fewer conflicts, with better sharing of plans and ideas.

The original meaning of *nemawashi* is to "loosen the roots," or in other words, to carefully dig a circle around the roots in order to preserve them when moving a plant or tree.

Similarly, when conducting *nemawashi* for a proposal, one is trying to carefully create a circle of consensus among the key people involved to move the proposal unscathed to the formal setting of a meeting.

□ 考慮 consideration
□ 会議の前に prior to the meeting
□ 調整する to adjust
□ 首尾よく行う do a thorough job
□ 紛糾する to become complicated

□ 〜するのはよくあること It is common to 〜
□ 〜といった or some such
□ そもそもの意味 original meaning
□ 人の輪をつくる create a circle of consensus

Harmony

「根回し」は今でも日本の組織のあちこちで実践されています。外国の人が「根回し」の外におかれないためには、日本人と、より気軽に接触し、時には夜、一緒にお酒を飲むなどして、日本人の輪の中に入ってゆくことが肝要です。

これは、日本では公式な場だけではなく、個々人のレベルでの密なコミュニケーションがいかに大切かを物語る、象徴的な概念であるともいえそうです。

Even now the use of *nemawashi* is quite common in organizations in Japan. It is important for non-Japanese to also move into "the circle of consensus" when conducting business in Japan by spending more time in *nemawashi* over drinks or in other informal settings.

This says just how important informal, one-on-one settings are in communicating in Japan. *Nemawashi* is indeed a representative concept of Japanese values.

□ あちこちで実践されている quite common
□ 外におかれる be left out of the party
□ 肝要な important
□ 密な one-in-one
□ いかに how
□ 象徴的な representative
□ 概念 concept

2
型
かた

Form,
Way of Doing Things

型
かた

「和」という価値観で、農耕社会を基軸とする日本社会でのコミュニケーションの方法について説明しました。そして、自分の考えや能力を強く主張することなく社会を運営してゆくために、日本人が発展させてきた価値観が、ここに紹介する「型」という考え方です。

古代から、農業での豊作を神に感謝し、人と人との絆を強くするために、人々は様々な儀式をつくってゆきました。その後、身分や階級制度が社会に浸透する中で、さらに人と人との上下関係を具体的に表すための作法やマナーが生み出されます。

儀式や作法は、全ての人がその様式に従うために、それぞれの「場」での行動様式、すなわち「型」が生み出され、それによって社会の多くの場面で、様々な「型」が尊重されるようになったのです。

今では、「型」は日本人の生活様式、行動のいたるところにみることができます。ビジネスでの名刺交換、相撲での取組前の儀式、そしてごく日常でいうならば、お酒の席での杯の受け方やつぎ方などが例です。

Form

We have already discussed how *wa* ("harmony") was an essential social value in the communication style of feudal Japan. Here we will introduce *kata* ("form"), another Japanese value that promotes social cooperation over one's individual thoughts or capabilities.

In ancient times, people in agricultural communities gave thanks to the gods, creating various ceremonies that helped to strengthen bonds with other people. Later, as a class system developed, additional forms of etiquette came into being as a means of expressing the difference in rank among people.

To ensure that all people would appropriately follow the various ceremonies and etiquette, the concept of *kata* developed, whereby a particular *kata* ("form") would be followed at a particular place and time.

Nowadays, one can see *kata* in action in all aspects of Japanese life. The exchange of name cards, the pre-bout rituals of sumo, even the relatively mundane act of pouring and receiving a cup of sake—these are all examples.

□ 農耕社会 feudal Japan
□ 豊作 rich harvest
□ 社会に浸透する develop
□ 生み出される come into being
□ ～によって whereby

□ いたるところに in all aspects
□ ごく日常の relatively mundane

Form, Way of Doing Things | *31*

また、武道や伝統の専門領域のことを習得するためには、まずそこで培われた「型」を学ぶことが要求されます。「型」をマスターしてこそ、人々は次のステップに進むことができるのです。「型」を習得するという価値観は、日本人が物事を進めるにあたって、どのように対処すべきかという方程式をまず理解しようとするのが重要です。まず、行動し、試行錯誤をしながら進めるのではなく、「いかに(how)」の答えを見つけてから進もうとする考え方を日本人は好むのです。

「型」は、日本人の行動様式、ビジネスの進め方を理解する上でも大切な価値観なのです。

In *budō* ("martial arts") or in other traditional disciplines, one must first cultivate *kata*. The more quickly one is able to master *kata*, the quicker one will advance to the next step. For the Japanese, before tackling a project, it is essential that they first understand the process by which that project will be completed. It is not proper to take random actions, trying to accomplish things through trial and error; rather one must first understand the answer to the question: How?

Kata is an important concept in understanding how the Japanese operate in business and in other fields.

□ 次のステップに進む to advance to the next step
□ 〜するのは重要だ It is essential that ~
□ 試行錯誤 trial and error
□ 理解する上で in understanding

Form, Way of Doing Things | *33*

修練

「型」を学ぶときは、何度も同じことを繰り返しながら、柔道での体の動きや習字での筆の使い方、あるいは踊るときの振る舞い方などを習得します。もちろん、「型」にはそれぞれ合理的な理由があったはずです。しかし、それがいかに合理的であるかを理解するためには、ただ黙々と「型」によって表現されるパターンを覚えてゆく必要があります。

教える者は、得てして理由を伝えることなく、教える者が納得するまで、学習者に「型」を教え込みます。日本には伝統的にフィードバックという文化がなく、学ぶ者は教える者を信じ、その指示に問いかけることなく従ってゆきました。

「型」の習得には時には何年もの修業期間が必要です。そしてしっかりと「型」を学んだ後に、はじめて学習者はその合理性に気付き、そこからさらに技量を発展させてゆくのです。

この「型」を学ぶ厳しい過程を「修練」といいます。そして、「修練」というものの考え方は、ビジネスのノウハウを習得してゆく上での、上司と部下の関係にもみてとることができるのです。フィードバックがなく、ただ厳しく指導する上司は、最近でこそ少なくなりました。とはいえ、今なお、欧米人が日本人を上司にもったとき、フィードバックの少なさに戸惑うことがよくあります。

確かに、このフィードバックの少ない日本流の指導方法は、欧米のマネージメントとは根本的に異なっているようです。

Discipline

When learning a new *kata* ("form"), one will repeat the same action numerous times, whether it is a judō throw or the strokes of a calligraphy brush or the steps of a dance. Of course there is ultimately a logic to all *kata*, but in order to truly understand that logic, it is necessary for the student to continue to silently repeat the action.

The teacher does not tell the student why something must be done in a certain way; he simply continues to have the student repeat the action until he, the teacher, is satisfied. In Japan traditionally there is no culture of "feedback." The student trusts the teacher and follows the directions of the teacher without questioning.

In certain cases, it may be necessary to spend many years in training to master *kata*. Only then, after the *kata* has been mastered, does the student really first understand the true logic of his movements, and then from there he may further develop his skill.

This demanding process of learning a *kata* is called *shūren*. *Shūren* may be seen in the business world in the relationship between subordinate and boss, although in recent years the example of the boss who manages his subordinates harshly without any feedback has become rarer. That said, Westerners who have Japanese bosses are still often puzzled by the lack of feedback.

It is true that this lack of feedback is different from the communication and management style in the West.

□ あるいは or
□ 振る舞い方 steps
□ 黙々と silently
□ 納得するまで until he is satisfied
□ 問いかける to question

□ みてとる to see
□ 最近でこそ although in recent years

Form, Way of Doing Things | 35

匠
たくみ

最近、日本では伝統的な「技」をもって工芸や手仕事に携わる人が見直されてきています。こうした人々のことを「匠」と呼びます。

「匠」は、長い年月をかけて「型」を習得し、そこからさらに「技」を磨いて、技能を極めた職人のことを意味しています。

細かい手仕事など、人間にしかできない技術をもって伝統的な作品を作る職人は、機械化と合理化の中で次第に廃れてゆきました。しかし、最近の日本の伝統的な職人芸を見直そうという動きの中で、各所で「匠」の「技」が再発見されてきています。

実は、自動車業界などの製造業においても、研磨など、人の勘や微細な技量を必要とする分野で、「技」をいかに次世代に伝えてゆくか試行錯誤の努力がなされています。

「匠」の「技」をいかに若い世代に伝えるかというとき、果たして伝統的な師匠と弟子との関係を今の若い世代が受け入れてゆけるのかという課題があるのです。師匠を常に尊敬し、文字通り人生を預けるようにして技術を磨くのか、それとも「スキル」として実用的な技術の習得に努めるのか。難しい選択といえましょう。

特に、日本の伝統的な会社が、国際環境で海外の人を育成するとき、日本流の師弟関係は通用しません。時代に合った、「匠」の「技」の伝承が求められているのです。

36 | 型 かた

Craft

Recently those involved in traditional handicrafts in Japan have come to be viewed in a new light. In Japanese, these people are said to have a *takumi* ("craft").

These craftsmen develop their *takumi* through many years of mastering a *kata* ("form"), followed by further polishing of their *waza* ("skill"). Such craftsmen, who create traditional items that can only be made by hand, have been dwindling in numbers in this age of continued industrialization and rationalization. However, as the products created by these craftsmen have been reevaluated in recent years, so also have the *takumi* these artisans possess.

In fact, in the automobile and other industries, efforts are being made through trial and error to pass on to the next generation grinding and other skills that require detailed handiwork and intuition.

In trying to pass on to the next generation various *takumi* and *waza*, there is the issue of whether or not younger people will accept the traditional teacher–student relationship. Will they respect their teacher, entrusting their lives to him as they polish their *waza*, or will they simply work to master a narrow skill? It is a difficult choice to make.

It is not possible to use this traditional teacher–student model when training people outside of Japan. In that case, a new model for *takumi* and *waza* must be used.

□ 携わる involved in
□ 見直される be reevaluated
□ 廃れる to dwindle
□ 必要とする to require
□ 努力がなされている efforts are being made

□ 〜を伝える pass on to 〜
□ 人生を預ける entrust one's life
□ 通用しない it is not possible to use

Form, Way of Doing Things | *37*

3

道
みち
Way

道

「型」が技術を学ぶための具体的なノウハウであるとすれば、「道」は「型」を学び、その技量を高めてゆくための精神的な価値観を示す言葉です。

「道」は「みち」と発音される場合と、中国語のdaoからの「どう」と発音される場合があります。「道」は英語のroadあるいはwayにあたり、人が歩き、車が通るところを指す言葉です。その「道」を人生になぞらえることは、欧米でもよくあることです。そして、日本では、「型」の学習を「道」になぞらえて考えます。「道」は人がしなければならないことを示す言葉として、人生の色々な場面での処し方、道徳律を示す言葉としても使用されているのです。

日本人は伝統的に「道」というコンセプトを好み、人としての生き方を語るときにこの言葉を使用します。たとえば、「人としての道をはずす」といえば、不道徳な生き方をしていることを示します。また、「道を極める」といえば、匠の境地に至り、その分野の極意を極めた達人となることを意味します。

したがって、日本人は、学習し、技を磨かなければならない事柄に「道」という言葉を頻繁に付加します。

華道といえば、生け花を習得するプロセスを指し、剣道はもっと直裁に日本流のフェンシングとしてスポーツの名前になっています。柔道も同様ですし、日本古来の宗教も神道といわれ、この場合は「しんとう」と発音されます。

「道」の考え方は、遠くに至るまで続く学習方法を示すことによって、そのhowに従って生きようとする日本人の文化背景に深く根ざした価値観であるといえましょう。

40 | 道 みち

Way, Road

If *kata* is the concrete know-how by which a skill is learned, then *michi* is the spiritual value by which that skill is further strengthened.

The Chinese character for *michi* can also be read as *dō* (from the Chinese "dao"). In English, *michi* would be translated as "way" or "road," the path used by a person to walk or by a vehicle to travel. The same as in Japanese for *michi*, the words "way" or "road" are often used in Western languages as metaphors for life. In Japan, *michi* is also often used as a metaphor for the process of learning various *kata* as one proceeds down the road of life, doing what one must to become a more virtuous person.

The Japanese have traditionally liked the concept of *michi* and will often use it when describing the type of life lead by a person. For example, if a person is leading an immoral life, they will say that that person is *fudōtoku* ("not on the road of virtue"). As another example, when a person pushes his skill to the utmost and is on the cutting edge of a field, the Japanese say that he is "taking the road to its ultimate destination" (*michi wo kiwameru*).

The word *michi* is therefore often used when the Japanese are describing circumstances where they must learn or polish a skill.

Kadō (written with the characters for "flower" and "way") is the art of flower arrangement; *kendō* ("sword" and "way") is the martial art of fencing; *jūdō* ("flexible" and "way") is another martial art; and *Shintō* ("gods" and "way"—here pronounced *tō*) is the native religion of Japan.

The concept of *michi* reflects the approach taken to learning since ancient times in Japan; it is a social value with deep roots in Japanese culture.

□ 具体的な concrete
□ なぞらえる to use something as a metaphor
□ 道をはずす lead an immoral life
□ 境地に至る to push one's skill to the utmost
□ 頻繁に often

□ 付加する to append
□ 〜に深く根ざした with deep roots in

道理

「道理」とは、ロジックを意味した言葉です。

「道理」の「理」という言葉は、「ことわり」ともよみ、それは物事の本来あるべき姿を示す言葉です。また、ロジックにかなった当然の帰結をも意味する言葉です。その言葉に「道」の概念が加わり「道理」となるわけで、それは、人が道徳律に従った行動をし、ロジックもしっかりとしていることを指し示すときに使用されるのです。

封建時代からずっと日本人が培ってきた価値観にそって、たとえば年上の人を敬い、師匠や上司に敬意を払って、それにふさわしい行動をすることは、日本では「道理に叶った」行動であるといわれます。

すなわち、単に理屈が通り、ロジックに支えられているのではなく、そこにしっかりとした道徳的なバックアップがあることが「道理」の意味するところなのです。そして、その道徳は、日本の伝統的な価値観に支えられているわけで、必ずしも万国全てに受け入れられるものではありません。

人生のあり方を示す「道」という価値観が、日本人のロジックの構成に大きく影響を与えている証拠が、この「道理」という言葉なのです。

Reason

The English translation for *dōri* would be "reason."

The Chinese character of *ri* in *dōri* is also read as *kotowari* and means the "proper structure" of things, or in other words, "reason" or "truth." By adding the character for *dō* ("way") to *ri*, we come up with *dōri*, or the proper "structure" of a person, with the concept of "reason" also clearly expressed.

In keeping with social values which have been cultivated since feudal times, the Japanese use the phrase *dōri ni kanatta* ("following reason") to describe the actions of a person who pays proper respect to his elders, teachers, or superiors.

In other words, it is not enough to simply put forth clever arguments; *dōri* requires that one must also have a moral backbone supporting one's words. As this morality is based on traditional values nurtured in Japan, it is not something that one can expect to be accepted in all countries around the world.

Proof that the social value of *michi*, or *dō*, is imbedded in the concept of reason can be seen in the very word *dōri*, which includes the character for *dō*.

□ あるべき姿 proper structure
□ 〜となる come up with
□ 封建時代 feudal times
□ 道理に叶った following reason
□ 意味するところ meaning

□ 〜に支えられている be based on 〜
□ 万国全て all countries round the world

Way | 43

武士道

「道」という概念を最も端的に表しているのが、封建時代に武士が自らのあるべき生き方として心に刻んでいた「武士道」という価値観です。

「武士道」については、明治時代の思想家であり外交官でもある新渡戸稲造が『武士道』という名著を残しています。

新渡戸稲造は、ちょうど欧米でのキリスト教のように、それを日本人の道徳律の源泉であるとして、封建時代から培ってきた日本人の価値観、善悪を判断する基準としての道徳律が「武士道」であると説いているのです。

武士のことを別のいい方で侍と呼び、そちらの方が欧米では有名になってしまいました。武士とは刀をもって戦い、時には主君や村や町を敵から守る人のことを指します。侍は、その武士が封建制度の枠組みにそって主君に仕えてゆく中で生まれた言葉です。

ちょうど西欧の騎士のように、主君に対して忠誠を誓い、必要とあれば命も捧げて主君とその領土を守り抜くことが侍の勤めでした。そのために常に精神的、肉体的な鍛錬を怠らず、死をも克服できる強い人格形成に努めることが、侍のあるべき姿とされたのです。こうした侍の人生観と、それに育まれた行動様式が武士の「道」、すなわち「武士道」なのです。

44 道みち

The Way of the Warrior

The concept of *michi,* or *dō,* was expressed in its purest form by *bushi* ("warriors") during the feudal period in the way of life known as *bushidō.*

The Meiji Era (1868–1912) philosopher and diplomat Nitobe Inazo wrote a well-known book entitled *Bushidō: The Soul of Japan.*

In this book, Nitobe made the argument that *bushidō* is to Japan as Christianity is to the West, in the sense that *bushidō* is the source of moral law in Japan, providing the basis for judging right and wrong.

Another expression for *bushi* is *samurai,* a word that has become better known in the West. The *bushi* fought with swords, and at times could be called on to protect their masters or villages or towns from enemies. The *samurai* were *bushi* who, in the feudal structure of the time, served their lords.

As with the knights of the West, the *samurai* swore allegiance to their lords and were prepared to sacrifice their lives in defense of him and his land. To fulfill their role, the *samurai* trained hard both physically and mentally to develop a fortitude that could withstand the constant threat of death. This way of viewing life and the actions which grew out of such a view were the *dō* ("way") which the *bushi* traversed; hence the word *bushidō.*

□ 端的に in its purest form
□ 名著 great book
□ ～であると説く make the argument that
□ 封建制度の枠組みにそって In the feudal structure of time

□ 命を捧げる sacrifice one's life
□ 強い人格形成に努める develop a fortitude
□ 人生観 way of viewing life

Way | 45

忠誠を貫くために常に何を学び、いかに振る舞うべきか。人の上に立つ身分である侍が常に心がけなければならない義務や掟はどのようなものか。「武士道」は、個人の欲望を抑え、質素な中で清廉に生き、死を畏れずに主君を守り抜くことの大切さを教えていました。そして、侍は、寡黙で、物事に動じる事なく、常に平常心で危急に対処する精神力が求められたのです。

現在でも日本には、個人の利益よりも会社の責務を優先し、だまって命ぜられた業務をこなすビジネスの環境が見受けられます。特に上に立つ者は、部下の過ちも自らの責任として引き受けようとすることを美徳とする風習が残っています。

若い世代にこの「武士道」が廃れてきたと嘆く年配の人も多くいます。そして、もちろん、昔でも現実が「武士道」の理想と乖離したことも多々ありました。

しかし、これからも日本人の価値観の一番奥底に、「武士道」的な発想が、時代によって変化しながらも、受け継がれていくのではないでしょうか。

46 道 みち

In the pursuit of loyalty, the *bushi* were always concerned about what to learn and how to act. As persons of higher rank than others, what type of responsibilities and rules did the *samurai* in fact have to keep in mind? *Bushidō* taught the importance of controlling individual desires, not fearing death, and leading a simple life of integrity as one protected one's lord. *Samurai* were also expected to be taciturn, unswayed by events around them, able to remain calm and respond to danger at any time.

In today's business world in Japan this way of thinking can still be found, as duty to one's company comes before individual profit, and company employees take care of requested assignments with few questions. It can also be seen in the case of managers who take responsibility for the mistakes of their subordinates.

Many older Japanese are disappointed that the younger generation has fallen away from the principles of *bushidō*. Of course, even in the past, the reality of *bushidō* was not always aligned with the ideal.

However, even as the times continue to change, it seems likely that *bushidō* will remain at the heart of Japanese social values.

□ ～を貫く in the pursuit of ~
□ 質素な simple
□ 寡黙 taciturn
□ 動じる to sway
□ 危急 danger

□ ～をこなす take care of
□ ～と乖離する not aligned with
□ 奥底 at the heart
□ ～ながらも even as

Way 47

業
ぎょう

「業」とは、直訳すればトレーニングということになるのでしょうか。しかし、その意味するところは、「克己心」を培うために日常的に厳しい義務を己に課してゆくことなのです。

それは、ちょうど僧侶が悟りを目指して行う修行に通じるものがあります。実際日本では、山奥の厳しい環境で修行をすることを、「業」を行うと表現します。

「型」を学ぶときの「修練」も、ある意味では「業」であるといえましょう。以前、アメリカ人の著者、ロバート・ホワイティングが日本の野球を単なるスポーツとしてではなく、剣道や柔道と同じく、野球道であると評論しました。

それは、日本人が野球の練習をするときに、ただ技能を磨くのではなく、野球場という自らを鍛える場への敬意を学ぶために行う清掃から、先輩への礼儀作法、さらに一見野球の技術とは関係のない禅寺での座禅まで、精神的な側面を極めて重くみるトレーニングを重ねていることを彼がみたからです。まさに、野球を極めるための「業」をしているのだと、ロバート・ホワイティングは思ったのでしょう。

「業」という精神修業の方法は、現在のビジネスでの新人研修にも多く取り入れられています。

「業」は日本人のトレーニングに関する考え方の基本にある価値観で、何かを成し遂げるための長い「道」を進む上で大切な考え方なのです。

Training

If one must translate *gyō*, the closest word in English would probably be "training." However, this would be "training" in the sense of tasking oneself with the demanding responsibility of working hard day-to-day to cultivate one's *kokkishin* ("self-denial").

Buddhist priests do such training when they are seeking enlightenment (*satori*). In Japan, when one does such tough training deep in the mountains, one is said to be "conducting *gyō*" (*gyō wo okonau*).

The *shūren* ("discipline") used when one is learning *kata* ("forms") may be said to be a type of *gyō*. Robert Whiting, an American author, has written that Japanese baseball is in fact not a sport but rather a discipline, *yakyūdō*, along the same lines as *kendō* or *jūdō*.

He points out that Japanese players do not simply practice baseball; rather they also place emphasis on the spiritual side in their training—paying respect to the ball field by keeping it clean, being properly deferential to their seniors, and even going so far as to sit in meditation in *Zen* temples. It must have been very clear to Whiting that the players were employing a particularly Japanese form of training, *gyō*, in order to reach the top of their game.

In today's business world, many aspects of *gyō* are also used in the mental or spiritual training of workers.

For the Japanese, *gyō* is an essential value in all training; it is an important aspect of the *michi* ("road") one travels in seeking to accomplish anything.

☐ 己に課す to task oneself
☐ 山奥 deep in the mountains
☐ 先輩 seniors
☐ 〜を重くみる to place enphasis on
☐ 極める to reach the top

☐ 精神修業 the mental or spiritual training
☐ 成し遂げる to accomplish

Way

求道

「業」を行い、自らが極めようとしている事柄に対して熱心に学習したり修行したりすることを「求道」と言います。

「道」を極めるために、しっかり修行し、自らを**律する**行為が「業」であるならば、そうした「業」を真摯に行う**心がけ**が「求道」の精神です。

「道」という価値観を重んずる日本人は、「道」を極めるためにいかに努力し、目標に向けて「修練」を重ねるかということに強い関心を示します。「道」を極めるためのこうしたプロセスへの美学がそこに**見受けられます**。

仮に結果が思わしくなくても、そこに至るプロセスにおいて努力を重ねていれば、人はそれを評価し尊敬します。「求道」の精神こそが、結果以上に求められているのです。

ある意味で、結果重視の欧米型のビジネス文化からみるならば、「求道」の精神やプロセスを重んずる日本人の行動様式は非合理的にみえるかもしれません。

しかし、日本人からみるならば、結果を得ることそのものよりも、努力することで得られる経験や精神的な**高み**のほうがより重要なのです。

Seeking the Truth

When one trains and studies hard to thoroughly master something, this is called *gudō* ("seeking the truth").

If one defines *gyō* as the act of doing such training in order to find one's way (*michi*), then one can think of *gudō* as the sincere spirit employed in doing one's *gyō*.

For the Japanese, who highly value the concept of *michi,* there is a strong interest in how one disciplines oneself as one works hard to find one's way and reach a goal. One can see the aesthetic of seeking one's way in the process itself.

Even if the results are not what were hoped for, people will positively judge the effort made in the process. It is precisely in the spirit of *gudō* that something more than simply results is expected.

From the perspective of Westerners, who place a heavy emphasis on results in their business culture, the spirit of *gudō*, with the importance placed on the process, must seem impractical.

However, from the Japanese perspective, the experience and the improvement in one's spirit gained through the effort are more important than the results.

□ 律する to discipline
□ 真摯に sincerely
□ 心がけ spirit
□ 見受けられる One can see
□ 思わしくない not what are hoped for

□ そのもの itself
□ 高み improvement

Way | *51*

その経験が培った強い精神力があれば、たとえそこでの結果が思わしくないとしても、他の「場」において、しっかりと物事に取り組むことができるというわけです。

武士道においても、もしその人が精神鍛錬をしっかりと行えば、結果は自ずとついてくると教えられます。

試合に勝つことは、訓練を重ねてきたことの、一つの結果に過ぎないというわけです。

Even if the results are not good in a particular situation, one will be able to better handle future situations, thanks to the stronger spirit that one has developed.

In *bushidō*, it was thought that if one trained properly to develop the proper spiritual power, then the results would take care of themselves.

In other words, coming out ahead in a competition is nothing more than one result of the training that has been done.

□ たとえ〜としても Even if ~

□ 結果はついてくる the results would take care of themselves

□ 〜に過ぎない nothing more than

4

気
(き)
Energy

気

「気」とは古代中国に生まれた概念で、この世にある目には見えないエネルギーの動きを意味します。

たとえば、会議をしているとき、お互いに意見が対立して、何も前に進まなかったとしましょう。そのとき、会議室の中になんとなく鬱々とした雰囲気が漂います。その雰囲気も「気」の一つです。

朝、澄んだ空気の中を歩いていると心が爽快になります。そんな気持ちを呼び起こす雰囲気も「気」なのです。

すなわち、「気」がよければ人は前向きで元気になり、「気」が悪ければ人は精神的にも肉体的にもくたびれてしまいます。

「気」の概念は古代の日本に伝わり、今でも日本人のものの考え方や判断の仕方に大きな影響を与えています。

「気」は場所や時間、あるいは人との関係やコミュニケーションの状況などによって様々に変化します。そして、「気」は人の心の中にもあり、その人の中によい「気」が充満していれば、仕事にも個人の生活にも充実感があるはずだと日本人は思うのです。

Energy

Ki, which is a concept developed in ancient China, describes the movement of unseen energy in our world.

For example, let's say that in a meeting there is a difference of opinion that prevents the discussion from moving forward. In that situation, a depressed atmosphere will envelop the conference room. That atmosphere is an example of one type of *ki.*

When one walks in a morning's clear air, one feels refreshed. The feelings brought forth in that case are an example of another type of *ki.*

In other words, if one encounters good *ki,* one feels energetic and positive, while if one encounters bad *ki,* one feels poorly and lacks energy both spiritually and physically.

Ki has been a concept in Japan since ancient times, and today it still has a large influence on how the Japanese think and view things.

Ki will change depending on the time and place, as well as the kind of relationship of the people involved and the circumstances of their communication. *Ki* is also found in people's hearts, and the Japanese believe that if a person is full of good *ki,* then he will be fulfilled in both his work and his personal life.

□ この世 our world
□ 目には見えない unseen
□ なんとなく for some reason
□ 鬱々とした depressed
□ 雰囲気が漂う an atmosphere envelopes

□ 爽快 refreshed
□ 呼び起こす to awake
□ くたびれる to get tired
□ 充満する to fill
□ 充実感がある to be fulfilled

また、多くの場合「気」は、自分の努力で変えることができるのです。たとえば「気」が悪いと意識したら、それをよくするために何をすべきか人は考えます。会議でよい結論がでず、**行き詰まったとき**、休憩をとって**気分転換をはかる**のも、「気」を変えてよいエネルギーを呼び込む**手段**といえましょう。

　「気」を読み取って、うまく対処できる人間が、より評価されるのです。「気配り」という概念は、まさにその時の「気」を理解して、相手に対する対応を考えることなのです。

　それはロジックではありません。それゆえに文化背景の違う欧米の人にとって、「気」の概念を理解することは大変なことかも知れません。

58 ｜ 気き

In most cases, one should be able to change one's *ki* through one's own efforts. For example, if one feels that one's *ki* is not good, then one should consider in concrete terms how to improve one's *ki*. If a meeting is not progressing well, then one might consider taking a break to change the atmosphere and generate better energy.

People who are capable of gauging *ki* and handling it in an appropriate way are highly thought of. The concept of *kikubari* ("sharing one's heart"). is indeed a case of understanding the *ki* of the moment and being attuned to the needs of other people.

The concept of *ki* is not necessarily logical. For Westerners, who have grown up with a different culture, *ki* may indeed be a foreign concept.

□ 行き詰る to go nowhere
□ 気分転換をはかる to create a diversion
□ 手段 technique
□ ～に対する to be attuned to ~
□ それゆえに therefore

□ ～にとって for

Energy | *59*

運気

「運気」とは、いわゆる占いの世界での運勢の動きを示す言葉です。西欧の占星術と同じように、中国や韓国、そして日本でも、星の動きやその人の生年月日、名前などを組み合わせた複雑な解析方法による占いが昔から存在します。

日本人は占いが好きで、テレビのワイドショーでは今日の運勢を占うコーナーがあり、繁華街には占い師がいて、手相や姓名判断などをみてもらおうと多くの人がやってきます。

「運気」は「気」の動きと深く関わっています。「気」の悪い状態におかれれば、その人の「運気」は下がり、やがて病気や何かのトラブルに巻き込まれるといわれています。

「気」とは見えないエネルギーですが、それは個人の中にもあれば、宇宙の動きにも関連しています。「運気」の強い人は、そうした「気」を前向きに取り込み、自らの気力を高め、強運を導き入れることができるというわけです。

日本には「病は気から」という言葉があります。この「気」はここで紹介する「気」のほかに、人の気持ちを示す「気」でもあるのです。つまり、精神状態がよくないと病の原因となるというのが、この言葉の意味するところです。

心の持ち方によって、人は様々な「気」を外に発することができます。したがって、前向きに物事を考えれば、自ずと病を克服し、強い運を呼び寄せることができるというわけです。

「運気」は自らの心の持ち方で大きく左右されるのです。

60 気

Fate

The word *unki* refers to the practice of fortune telling. Like the astrology of the West, a method of predicting one's fate based on a complex analysis of the stars or one's birthdate or name has existed in China, Korea, and Japan since ancient times.

Fortune telling is popular in Japan, with many people watching featured sections on TV shows or going to street stalls in the cities for palm reading and analysis of names.

Unki has a strong connection with the movement of *ki*. When the *ki* is not good, one's *unki* will be in a downward trend, and it is at such times that it is easy to become sick or run into trouble of some sort.

Ki is an energy that can not be seen, existing in individuals and also in connection with the movement of the universe. People with a strong fate are those who are able to take hold of that *ki* and through their own efforts pull that energy into their lives.

In Japanese the word for illness (*byōki*) is made up of the Chinese characters for "sick" (*byō*) and *ki*. In addition to the meaning of *ki* introduced here ("energy"), *ki* can also mean "feelings," as in the *ki* of *kimochi*. In other words, one's poor emotional condition may become a cause of illness.

Depending on one's emotional state, one will emit various types of *ki*. If one is in a positive state of mind, one may be able to overcome an illness on one's own and bring good luck to oneself.

One's *unki* can change significantly depending on one's attitude.

□ いわゆる so-called
□ 組み合わせる to combine
□ 関わる to have a connection
□ やがて at such times
□ 前向きに positively

□ 発する to emit
□ 〜に左右される to depend on

Energy | *61*

殺気

「気」の概念を理解するのに「殺気」は最適な概念かも知れません。
その昔、よく訓練された武士が殺意をもった相手に出会うと、相手が刀を抜いて挑みかかる前に、その殺意を感じることができたといわれていました。その殺意が空気のように漂っていることを「殺気」というのです。すなわち、言葉や明快な行動に表さなくても、そこで醸し出される雰囲気や、微妙な表情や仕草から、その人の発する「気」を読み取ることができるのです。

すでに何度か言及していますが、日本人は言葉の外にある意味を読んでコミュニケーションしようと試みます。昔、修行を重ねた武士は、相手が険しい表情をしたり、睨みつけたりという仕草をしていなくても、その人から「殺気」を感じ、心の中で闘う準備をしていたといわれています。

人の発する「気」は、相手に伝わり、相手はそれに対応して身構えることによって、自らの意思を無言で相手に伝えます。すなわち、「気」を交換することで、相対するふたりは互いに意思を伝達するのです。

現代社会において、これは漫画や映画の世界でのことですが、日本人は今でも言葉にして出すことなく、相手に気持ちを伝えようと期待することは事実です。ですから、外国の人からみれば、日本人が本当は何が言いたいのかよくわからないという戸惑いが生まれてしまうのです。

62 気

Sensing Danger

Sakki is another concept that is helpful to know in order to understand the concept of *ki*.

In the old days, it was said that a well trained samurai could sense the intent of someone to make an attempt on his life even before his opponent had drawn his sword. That sense in the air is what is known as *sakki* ("sensing danger"). In other words, even without words or clear actions, the atmosphere and subtle facial expressions or movements would allow the well trained samurai to read the *ki* of his opponent.

As we have already explained a number of times, the Japanese will try to communicate in ways other than through words. Even if his opponent were not glaring at him with a severe expression, the well-trained samurai would "sense danger" and make his mental preparations for a fight.

The *ki* one emits is sent to the person one is with, and that person in turn readies himself so that one can now send his message to the other person without using words. In other words, by exchanging *ki*, two people are able to express their wills to each other.

In the modern world, this would be the stuff of comics or movies, but it is a fact that even now the Japanese expect to be able to express their feelings to others without using words. It is because of this that non-Japanese people are puzzled and have a difficult time trying to understand what the Japanese are saying.

□ その昔 in the old days
□ 挑みかかる to attack
□ 醸し出す to create an atmosphere
□ 言及する to explain
□ 試みる to try

□ 相対する to face
□ 期待する to expect

Energy | *63*

空気

「空気」は単に気体のことだけを意味しません。英語でも、「空気」は雰囲気などを示すときに使われる言葉です。

そして、日本語の場合も「空気を読む」という言葉があるように、人がコミュニケーションをするにあたって、そこでの雰囲気や様子が醸し出す状況を「空気」という言葉で表現します。

「空気」の「空」は、何もないからっぽな状態を示す漢字です。そのからっぽな状態に「気」が混ざり、「空気」となるのです。言葉を換えれば、「空気」は単なる気体ではなく、そこに充満する様々なエネルギーをすべて包括したものということになります。

そこに充満しているのが、どのような「気」なのかを察知し、それをもとに適切に物事に対処することは、日本人が常に心掛けている処世術ともいえましょう。

したがって、「空気」の概念は、第1章で紹介した「場」とも関連します。人と人が集まるタイミングや組み合わせによって、その場その場で様々な雰囲気が生まれます。すなわち、「場」に充満する空気を読み、たとえば話したい話題を予定通りに話すのか、それとも控えるのかといった判断をすることが、コミュニケーション上大切な戦略となるのです。

「気」は人と人とが交流する中で生み出されるエネルギーです。したがって、「場」や人の立場などを理解し、よりよい「気」をつくろうと多くの日本人は考えているのです。

Air, Atmosphere

Kūki ("air") is not simply a physical phenomenon. In English as well, "air" is also used to describe the atmosphere of a situation.

As in the Japanese phrase *kūki wo yomu* ("reading the air"), the conditions that have brought about a particular atmosphere or situation are said to be the *kūki*.

The Chinese character of *kū* in *kūki* is the character for "sky" and also means "empty." The character for *ki* is combined with the character for "sky" or "empty," to form *kūki*, or "air." Putting it another way, *kūki* is not merely a physical phenomenon; it also includes all of the various energies that inundate a particular situation.

As part of getting along in life, the Japanese will always try to determine what particular energies (*ki*) are coming to play in a situation and do their best to take appropriate action based on that.

The concept of *kūki* is therefore related to the concept of *ba* ("place") introduced in Chapter 1. Depending on the timing and combinations of when and where people get together, various types of atmosphere will be created. For example, as part of one's communication strategy, it is important to decide whether or not to bring up a particular subject based on the *kūki* of that *ba* ("place").

Ki is the energy that is created by the interchange between people. Therefore, most Japanese feel that it is important to do their best in understanding the circumstances of the people around them in order to create good *ki*.

□ 〜にあたって upon doing
□ からっぽな empty
□ 言葉を換えれば to put it another way
□ 包括する to include
□ 察知する to determine

□ 処世術 social politics
□ その場その場で situation by situation
□ 予定通りに as planned

Energy | 65

5 節 ふし Period

節と節目

「型」や「道」という価値を重んずる日本人は、常に自らがどの位置にあるかを知るためのマイルストーンを大切にします。このマイルストーンを表す言葉が「節」なのです。「節」は「せつ」とも「ふし」とも読みます。

「節」とは「節目」のことで、一年の「ふしめ」である四季のことを「節」の文字を使って季節と呼んだり、人生の大きな転換期を、人生の「節目」という風に表現します。

「節目」には始まりと終わりがあります。節のコンセプトを知るために、竹をイメージしてみてください。竹には「節」があり、その成長した節が重なって、一本の竹となっています。その一本の竹を人生、あるいは何かを学ぶプロセスと考えてみると、それぞれの「節」がいかに大切で、一つ一つの「節」がなければ竹は上に伸びないことが理解できるでしょう。

「道」を極めるにあたって、この「節」の連続性がいかに保たれ、一つずつの「節」の始まりと終わりをしっかりと意識し、次の「節」につなげるかが、物事を学び、人生を送る基本であるという価値観が「節目」には込められているのです。

Period

For the Japanese, who place much weight on the values of *kata* ("form") and *michi* ("way"), it is important to always take note of milestones. In Japanese, the Chinese character *setsu*, also read as *fushi*, expresses this concept of milestone.

The character of *setsu* is used with the *ki* of *shiki* ("four seasons") to make the word *kisetsu* ("season"). Again, the same character, this time read as *fushi*, is used in the word *fushime* to indicate an important transition point in a person's life.

A *fushime* ("period") has a beginning and an end. Let's use the image of bamboo to help us better understand the concept of *fushi*. A bamboo stalk has *fushi* ("nodes"), and the growth from node to node is what eventually results in a fully grown stalk. It is the same with one's life or with the process of learning something: each period is important and builds on the previous period; one cannot proceed to the next period without the last.

When seeking to master something, it is critical that continuity be preserved and that the beginning and end of each period be consciously recognized and connected with the next period, as part of the basic values of one's life. This is inherent in the concept of *fushime*.

□ 自ら oneself
□ 節 node, period
□ 転換期 transition point
□ 〜という風に like this
□ 連続性 continuity

□ 人生を送る to live a life
□ 込める to suggest

「節目」を重んずる日本人が、変化するときに単に未来に向かわずに、それまでお世話になった人に敬意を表したり、しっかりと挨拶をしたりすることは、欧米に人からみると、時には儀式ばってみえるかもしれません。

しかし、竹の解説からもおわかりのように、下の「節」を大切にしない限り、竹は上の「節」をつくり、伸びていかないのです。

次の始まりに向かうためにも、過去をしっかりと見つめ直すということが、「節」という概念が示す倫理観なのです。

From the point of view of Westerners, it must sometimes seem that the Japanese are simply enacting superfluous ceremonies when they mark the end of a period by going to the trouble of making various greetings and thanking people, rather than just moving on.

But for the Japanese it is a matter, of making sure that the last *fushi* is properly taken care of, like the bamboo, in order to ensure the growth of the next.

The ethics of *fushi* are clearly evident in this act of carefully considering what has happened in the past before moving on to something new.

☐ お世話になる to receive a favor
☐ 〜ばってみえる to look like
☐ おわかりにように as you can see
☐ 〜しない限り unless one does
☐ 倫理観 ethical sense

有終

「有終」とは終わりをしっかりと意識するという価値観です。多くの場合、「節」あるいは「節目」に示される倫理観を最も端的に表した言葉が、「有終の美」です。

たとえば、会社を辞めて、次のチャンスに向けて旅立つとき、人はまさに「節目」を経験します。その「節目」を大切にして、未来へ向かうために、辞めていく会社で最後の日までしっかりと働きます。そしてお世話になった人への挨拶を忘れず、**後任に引き継ぎ**をして、時には自分の机や周囲の掃除までして会社を去ることが、「有終の美」の価値観なのです。

この考え方は日常生活でもみることができます。ホテルや旅館に宿泊したとき、旅立つ前に部屋や布団を簡単に片付けたりする**行為**も「有終の美」の一例です。

「立つ鳥跡を濁さず」ということわざがあります。これは、水鳥は飛び立つとき池を濁すことなくきれいに飛び立つという意味から、旅立つとき、またはその場を去るとき、後の人のためにもその場所を美しく保って去ってゆこうということを意味します。

「有終の美」は、このことわざにもつながる、過去から未来への人や社会の繋がりをしっかりと意識するための倫理観といえるのではないでしょうか。

Beautiful Ending

The word *yūshū* expresses the social value of coming to terms with an ending. In many cases, the ethical values of *fushi* or *fushime* can be expressed most directly in the phrase *yūshū no bi* ("beautiful ending").

For example, when a person quits his job and moves on to his next opportunity, he is clearly experiencing a *fushime* ("transition point"). "A beautiful ending" can be seen in this case, as the person treats the transition with respect, working hard up through the last day, making proper greetings to his colleagues, briefing his replacement, and even in the way he cleans out his desk before leaving his job.

We can also see this way of thinking in everyday life. Tidying up the room and putting the futon away before leaving a hotel or Japanese inn would be another example of a "beautiful ending."

There is a saying in Japan that "a bird taking off doesn't muddy the waters." In the same way that a water bird takes flight from a pond without disturbing the water, so should a person, be careful to put things in order so as not to inconvenience those left behind.

The ethical sense behind a "beautiful ending" is also seen in this saying, as one properly connects the people and events of one's past with one's future.

□ 後任 replacement
□ 引き継ぎ taking over charge
□ 簡単に shortly
□ 行為 act
□ 濁す to muddy

□ 飛び立つ to take flight

Period

節度

　竹の「節」の一つ一つを人生になぞらえ、大切に生きてゆこうという発想は、自らが現在留まっている「節」の中で、自分を整え、その「節」を破ることなく、次の「節」に旅立つまでしっかりと謙虚に自分を磨こうという価値観を導きます。その価値観を「節度」と呼びます。「和」の章でみてきた、「謙遜」や「謙譲」という価値観が融合して「節度」という意識となってここで活きてくるのです。

　敢えて自らを強くアピールすることなく、現在おかれている位置や立場を理解し、その日々の積み重ねから自身が成長してゆくことが「節度」という価値観です。

　ダイナミックに変化する現代において、封建時代から培われてきたこの価値観は時代にそぐわないかもしれません。

　よく、日本人は何を考え、何がしたいのかわからないという苦情を（外国の人から）聞きますが、その背景には、日本人が常に「節度」という価値観を持ち、自らの考えや思いを強く主張することを控えようという意識があるからかもしれません。

　しかし、「節度」という価値観のよい面は、常に人に対して感謝や尊敬の念をもって接する心構えでしょう。

74　節 ふし

Restraint

Just as each node in a bamboo stalk is like each period in one's life, so it is that one must also do the utmost to train and prepare oneself while one is in a particular period of life, while also being careful not to go on to the next stage before one is ready. This value is called *setsudo* ("restraint"). In the chapter on *wa* ("harmony"), we discussed the value of modesty (*kenson*, *kenjō*), and here we will see how modesty is reflected in the concept of *setsudo*.

Rather than seeking individual recognition, *setsudo* means working hard day-to-day to improve oneself within one's current position and situation.

This value, which has been cultivated in Japan since feudal times, may not fit with today's world, in which dynamic change is the norm.

Non-Japanese may often complain that they don't know what the Japanese are thinking or what they want to do. *Setsudo* may be behind this, as the Japanese will refrain from giving strong opinions with this value in mind.

On the other hand, the good aspects of *setsudo* are the gratitude and respect always paid to other people.

☐ 謙虚 humility, modesty
☐ 導く to lead
☐ 融合する to blend
☐ 活きてくる be in effect
☐ 敢えて to dare to do

☐ 積み重ね buildup
☐ そぐわない not fit with
☐ よい面 good aspect
☐ 接する to contact

Period | *75*

現代のビジネス社会において、いかにチームワークをもってプロジェクトを進めてゆくかというテーマは大切です。そのとき、相手の立場を考え、相手に敬意を表しながら「節度」あるアプローチをとれば、多くの場合、対立がシナジーへと変化するかもしれません。

　価値観は古くなるのでも、的はずれになるのでもありません。むしろ、価値観にとらわれ形骸化した行動が、価値観そのものを古くさくしてしまうのです。

　そうした意味では、「節度」という価値観のよい面を見直してみるのも、必要なのではないでしょうか。

In today's business world, the amount of teamwork that can be brought to bear on a project is very important. If an approach employing *setsudo* is used, one in which the position of other people is carefully considered and the proper respect is paid to them, then in a surprisingly large number of cases it may be possible to change conflict into synergy.

It is not a matter of values becoming old and irrelevant on their own. Rather, it is a matter of the essence of values being lost due to the changing attitudes and actions of people.

In that sense, it may be necessary to acknowledge once again the good aspects of *setsudo*.

☐ テーマ theme
☐ アプローチをとる to approach
☐ シナジー synergy
☐ 的はずれ irrelevant
☐ 形骸化する to become a mere shell

けじめ

「有終の美」の概念でもおわかりのように、日本人は一見非合理的にすら見えるほどに、物事の終わりを大切にし、「節目」をしっかりと意識しながら未来へ向かうことをよしとします。

この物事の変化にあたって、しっかりと「節」の価値観に従って行動することを日本人は「けじめ」といいます。

たとえば、人が罪を犯した場合、ただ逃げ隠れするのではなく、あえて警察に自首し、刑に服することがあります。この行為を日本では、「けじめ」をつけるといいます。すなわち、自らの行動に対してしっかりと責任をとり、それにふさわしい態度や対応をすることが「けじめ」なのです。

現在でも、日本人は「けじめ」を常に意識しているようです。

たとえば、ビジネスの世界で、会社が不良品を製造したり、業績が低迷したりという厳しい状態におかれたとき、日本では会社の経営者が責任をとって辞任することが頻繁にあります。直接その人が原因で起きた問題でなくとも、責任者として、会社が未来へ向かうための「けじめ」をつけるのです。

物事が変化する節目に、いかに「けじめ」をつけるか。日本人はそこでの行動に注目して、その人物を評価するわけです。

Marking a Break

As seen in the concept of *yūshū no bi* ("a beautiful ending"), the Japanese can appear impractical in how they treat endings, taking due note of *fushime* ("transition points") before moving on to a new stage of life.

Kejime is the action one takes in accord with the concept of *fushi* ("period") as one marks a change in one's life.

For example, if one commits a crime and, instead of running away, one turns oneself into the police and submits to the appropriate punishment, in Japan this is called *kejime wo tsukeru* ("marking a break"). In other words, having the right attitude to take responsibility for one's actions is an important aspect of *kejime*.

The Japanese today remain very aware of the concept of *kejime*.

For example, it is quite common in Japan for the chief executive of a company to resign if his company has manufactured and sold defective goods. Even if the executive was not the direct cause of the defective goods, as the head of the company, it is incumbent on him to "mark a break" (*kejime wo tsukeru*) and take responsibility. For the Japanese, a person will be judged on how sincerely he "marks the break" during such a transition point (*fushime)* in his life.

□ 〜にすら見える can appear to be
□ 罪を犯す to commit a crime
□ 逃げ隠れする to run away and then hide oneself
□ 自首する to turn oneself into the police

□ 刑に服する to submit to the punishment
□ 低迷する to hover at a low level
□ 〜でなくとも even if it is not

Period | *79*

6 情
じょう
Feelings

情
じょう

「情」とは人の思いや感情を表す漢字です。

人の喜びや悲しみ、楽しみや苦しみを生み出す心のエネルギーを、日本人は「情」という言葉で言い表すのです。

よく、欧米の人が、日本の映画やテレビドラマは、感情表現の場がしつこく、ウエットすぎると批判します。その一つの理由として、日本人はジェスチャーや言葉を使って、感情を強く表現しないため、どうしても感情表現の場が長くなってしまうことが挙げられます。

恋人同士の別れの場を表現するときに、「愛しているよ。またすぐ逢いたい」と言えばすむ場面を、じっと涙をこらえて、目頭がすこし潤んできたときに、恋人を乗せた列車が出発するというように、むしろ言葉を交えずに表現したほうが、日本人の心に響いてくるのです。

特に、言葉はできるだけ少ない方が、**説得力がある**とするコミュニケーションスタイルをもつ日本人にとっては、言葉に表さない「情」を知覚することが、相手を理解する大切な要因となるのです。

このコミュニケーションスタイルが、日本人特有の「情」への価値観を育みました。すなわち、「情」は言葉に表さない人間の気持ちへの美学によって支えられた価値観なのです。

日本人は、「情」を感じるとき、相手に対して何かしてあげなければというモチベーションを**抱き**ます。そうしたモチベーションへの期待が、日本人特有の人間関係における**紐帯を育む**わけです。そしてビジネスであろうが個人であろうが、「情」を感じ合うとき、お互いに**打ち解け合って**話ができるのです。日本人特有の身近な人への甘えの構造がそこに見えてくるのです。

82 | 情 じょう

Feelings

Jō is the Chinese character for "feelings."

The Japanese express the energy created by such emotions as happiness, sadness, pleasure, and distress in the word *jō*.

Westerners often criticize Japanese movies or television dramas for being too emotional. One reason that can be given for this is that the Japanese tend to express their emotions indirectly rather than by using a lot of words or gestures; this means that it takes longer for such emotional scenes to be played out.

When two lovers part at a train station, for example, rather than simply saying, "I love you; I want to see you again soon," it is more emotional for the Japanese to play out the scene without words, with tears slowly building in the eyes and then trickling down the cheeks as the train leaves.

Particularly for the Japanese, whose communication style uses as few words as possible, it is critical when trying to understand another person to grasp the *jō* that is being expressed nonverbally.

It is this communication style that brought about the Japanese value of *jō*. In other words, it is the beauty of nonverbal human emotions that brings true life to this value.

When the Japanese feel *jō*, that is when they are most motivated to act. It is in turn this motivation to act, generated by *jō*, which creates the bonds of *ningen kankei* ("human relationships"), which are so important to the Japanese. It is here, too, that one can see the concept of *amae* ("dependency") in relationships with those to whom one is close.

☐ しつこい persistent
☐ どうしても unavoidably
☐ じっと quietly
☐ できるだけ as much as possible
☐ 説得力がある eloquent

☐ 抱く to hold
☐ 紐帯を育む to create the bonds
☐ AであろうがBであろうが whether A or B
☐ 打ち解け合って confidentially

人情

「情」という価値観をもっと端的に示しているのが「人情」という価値観です。洋の東西を問わず、人は誰でも親しい人に対して愛情を抱いています。また、めぐまれない人に接すれば、たいていの人には同情心がうまれます。この、他の人に対する個人的な感情を「人情」といいます。

たとえば、刑事裁判で、被告人が不幸な境遇にあったがために罪を犯したであろうと思われる場合、判事が軽い判決を下すことがあります。この場合、判事は「人情」によって心を動かされたとされ、人々はその判決に拍手するというわけです。

こうした話はよく時代劇の題材になります。「人情」によってビジネスや公の決済が影響を受けることは、日本ではむしろよいこととされているのです。状況によっては、「情」を加えることはむしろプラスなのです。

実は、日本人は、「ビジネスはビジネス」として、個人の「情」とビジネスを切り離すべきものだという考えになかなか馴染めません。本来は客観的に意見を交換し、判断を行うべきビジネスでのやりとりが、日本では「ハートとハート」のやりとりとして受け取られ、それがもとで人間関係が上手くいかなくなったり、取引が不調におわることもあるのです。

84 情 じょう

Personal Feelings

Ninjō is the value of *jō* ("feelings") expressed in a more direct manner. It is the willingness to embrace the love of all people without question as to their nationality. It also means that there is a sympathy for those whom one comes into contact with who have not been so fortunate in their lives. These emotions that one has for others are called *ninjō*.

For example, if a court is trying a criminal, the judge may give a lighter sentence if the person in question committed the crime due to the unfortunate circumstances of his environment. In that case, it would be said that the judge had been moved by *ninjō* and people would applaud his decision.

This type of story is often seen in *jidai geki* ("samurai tales"). In other words, when *ninjō* moves a person to be generous in making a business or public service decision, this is considered a good thing in Japan; and depending on the situation, the more generous the better.

It is true that it is difficult for most Japanese to accept the idea that "business is business" and separate their personal feelings from business. Although business should be conducted in a manner in which ideas are objectively exchanged and judgments made on that basis, in Japan it is instead common to conduct business on a "heart-to-heart basis," and this can often lead to broken relationships and bad business deals.

□ 洋の東西を問わず without question as to their nationality
□ めぐまれない not been so fortunate
□ たいていの most
□ 〜がために due to

□ 馴染む to accept
□ それがもとで on that basis
□ 不調におわる to lead bad business deals

Feelings | *85*

もちろん、日本でもビジネスと個人の「情」とを混同してはいけないという道徳律は存在します。それだけに、人は反対意見を述べたりするときは、「人情」を意識し、気を使い、相手の立場をたてながら表明するのです。

　その表明の仕方自体が、欧米の人からみると、ビジネスと個人の「情」とが混在しているようにみえることもあるようです。

Of course in Japan, the principle of not mixing business with one's personal feelings also exists. When one is faced with someone taking an opposing position, however, one takes *ninjō* into account and is careful to do what one can to accommodate that person.

It is this very tendency of Japanese to take *ninjō* into account in such cases that apparently leads Westerners to believe that Japanese are mixing business and their personal feelings.

□ 混同する to mix up

□ それだけに for that reason

□ 述べる to state

□ 立場をたてる to show respect to someone's situation

□ ～自体 itself

Feelings | *87*

義理

「義理」とは、人と人とが人間関係を維持してゆくための義務や務めを意味する言葉です。

たとえば、ある人に大変お世話になった場合、その人に対して「義理」があると人はいいます。そこで生まれる義理を意識して、受けた恩恵に報いることが道徳的に求められているわけです。

日本の場合、この人と人との縛りが伝統的に強かったといえましょう。特に、江戸時代に代表される封建時代には、身分や性別、そして年齢など、様々な立場での役割が厳しく設定されていました。そして、役割を逸脱することや、自らの立場を超えて行動することは禁じられていたのです。

したがって、「義理」に縛られながら、その縛りを超えた人と人の「情」との間に挟まれて葛藤するテーマが、歌舞伎や文楽などの伝統芸能でよく取り上げられました。たとえば、親の「義理」に縛られて婚約させられた娘と、その娘に恋する若者の物語などが、それにあたります。「義理」と「人情」というテーマです。

ごく日常的な「義理」といえば、夏や年の暮れに、仕事上あるいはふだんの付き合いでお世話になった人に贈り物をしたり、挨拶にいったりする習慣があります。今でこそ少なくなりましたが、上司が引っ越しをするときに、部下がそれを手伝うといった習慣も挙げられます。

88　情 じょう

Obligation, Duty

Giri means the responsibility and effort that go into maintaining a relationship between one person and another.

For example, if one is indebted to another for a favor done, then it is said that one has *giri* to the other person. In that case, Japanese ethics require that one be well aware of the *giri* incurred and repay the favor.

In Japan this type of connection from person to person has traditionally been strong. Especially during the feudal Edo Era, one's position was strictly fixed according to one's rank, sex, age, and so on. It was not possible to deviate from one's rank or make an attempt to better oneself within society.

Because of this, conflicts between one's obligations (*giri*) and one's feelings (*ninjō*) were a common theme in the traditional performing arts such as the *kabuki* or *bunraku* ("puppet theatre"). An example of such a conflict would be a daughter who became engaged to one man to fulfill her *giri* to her father, while her true affections (*ninjō*) were for another young man. This would be a classic *giri–ninjō* theme.

In terms of everyday life, an example of *giri* would be giving gifts and making the rounds of greetings during the summer and at the end of the year to those whom one is indebted to for social or business favors. Another example, which is rare nowadays, would be for subordinates in a company to help their boss move.

☐ 維持する to maintain
☐ 報いる to repay
☐ 縛り connection
☐ 逸脱する to deviate
☐ 葛藤する to undergo a conflict

☐ 暮れ end
☐ 今でこそ nowadays

Feelings | *89*

多くの場合、「義理」はこうした上下関係での道徳律と深く関わっています。上司にお酒に誘われて、恋人とのデートの約束をどうしようかと迷うのも、**現代版**の「義理」と「人情」といえましょう。

　最近は、こうした場合、若い人は「人情」を**優先する**と、**年輩の人**はぼやいているのもまた事実なのです。

90　情 じょう

As in these cases, *giri* often has a strong connection to the ethics of relationships between those in higher and lower positions. It might be said that a modern version of a *giri–ninjō* conflict would be for a boss to invite one out for a drink on a night when one already had a date set with one's girlfriend.

It is a fact that older people today are not happy with the way that younger people tend to put *ninjō* ahead of *giri*.

□ 現代版 modern version
□ Aを (Bより) 優先する put A ahead of B
□ 年輩の人 older people
□ ぼやく to grumble

恩

　「義理」という考え方に最も影響を与えるのが「恩」という価値観です。

　封建時代には、君主は自らの部下である侍に俸禄を与え、その侍の身分を保障します。その地位は、その侍一代ではなく、代々受け継がれることが普通でした。

　この身分と生活の保障を君主から受けることが、侍にとっての「恩」です。侍はその受けている「恩」に報いるために、時には命をかけて君主に仕えなければなりません。すなわちそれが侍の「義理」というわけです。

　現在でも、「あの人には恩がある」と人はよくいいます。自分を育ててくれた親への「恩」、知識を与えてくれた教師への「恩」、そしてスキルを教えてくれた上司への「恩」などがそれにあたります。

　人は「恩」に対して、それに報いるように努力することが求められます。

　「恩」と「義理」との関係は、一時的なものではなく、多くの場合一生その人の人間関係に影響を与えます。昔は「恩」を忘れることは、最も非道徳的なこととして、非難されていたのです。

92　情 じょう

Social Debt

The social value known as *on* has heavily influenced the concept of *giri* ("obligation").

In the feudal period, a lord would pay his samurai a stipend and guarantee their position in society. It was the usual practice to guarantee that rank not just to that particular samurai, but to his descendants as well.

Having received a position and the guarantee of a living, the samurai would have incurred *on*, and in order to repay that social debt, the samurai would loyally serve his lord, at times having to put his life on the line. In other words, this was the samurai's *giri* ("obligation").

Even today, people often speak of "having *on*" to a particular person. Common examples would be the *on* that is incurred by a child to his parent, or a student to his teacher, or an employee to his boss.

It is expected that those who incur *on* will make efforts to repay it. In most cases, *on* and *giri* are lifelong obligations, not something which affects one only for the short-term. In the old days, forgetting to repay one's *on* was considered a very unethical act and would be heavily criticized.

□ 君主 load
□ 俸禄 stipend
□ 保障する to guarantee
□ 一代 one generation
□ 代々 layeredly

□ 一生 lifelong

日本人の心の中に深く残る「恩」という発想は、日本人がビジネスの上でも単にビジネスライクに物事を進めるのではなく、個人的な感情で判断をする原因の一つにもなっています。たとえば、「恩」のある人の子供だからということで、昇進や就職に手を加えることも時にはあり、それが様々な不正の原因となることもあるのです。

逆に、あの人には「恩」があるからということで、その人が死んだ後も、その子供や遺族の相談にのろうとする行為は、美徳であるともいえるでしょう。

「恩」という発想には、こうした功罪両面があるようです。

94　情 じょう

The concept of *on*, which is so deeply rooted in the character of the Japanese, is one reason why they are not able to take a more "business-like" approach to business, instead allowing personal feelings to affect their judgments. For example, inequities often result from giving favorable consideration for hiring or promotion to the child of someone to whom one has incurred *on*.

On the other hand, it is a thing of beauty to see someone reach out to assist the child or other family members of someone to whom one has incurred *on* after that person has died.

In this way, the concept of *on* would appear to have both merits and demerits.

□ 深く残る to be deeply rooted
□ 手を加える to give favorable consideration
□ 相談にのる to provide consultation
□ 功罪両面 both merits and demerits

Feelings | *95*

内と外

　人と人との複雑なしがらみの中で、その人の「情」と「義理」との関係がわかり、心を許して話ができる信頼関係が構築されたとき、その人は自分の人間関係の「内」にいると考えられます。

　たとえば、家族や会社の親しい同僚は「内」の関係で、そこに入らない人は「外」の人と捉えられます。「外」の人とは、ある程度お互いがよく知り合うまで、率直な付き合いを控えるのです。

　この「内」と「外」との境界線は、その人のおかれている立ち位置の違いによって変化します。たとえば、同じ村の人でも、家族からみると「外」の人ですが、違う村の人と比較すれば、「内」の人となります。外国の人を「外人」と呼びますが、この場合は日本を「内」と捉えているので、外国は「外」に他ならないのです。すなわち、「外人」とは「外の人」という意味なのです。

　複雑な人間関係から発生する齟齬や軋轢といったリスクを軽減するために、日本人は伝統的に「内」と考える相手に対してのみ、本当の思いや情報を共有する傾向にあります。

　「内」に迎えられるためには、何よりも、お互いを公私ともによく知り合う必要があります。そして、「情」をもって話し合える関係になれば、「内」に入った仲間として情報が共有されるのです。

Inside and Outside, Social Circle

When one is able to navigate the *shigarami* ("barriers") of a relationship and understand the particulars of *jō* ("feelings") versus *giri* ("obligations") to the point that one can let one's guard down and truly trust that person, then it is said that that person is *uchi* ("inside").

For example, a person who is not within one's family or close associates at one's company would be considered to be *soto* ("outside"), and one would have some reserve in dealing with that person until one got to know the person better.

How to distinguish between *uchi* and *soto* depends on the situation in question. For example, people in the same village who are not in the same family would be considered *soto* in terms of family, but those same people would be considered *uchi* in terms of the village versus people from outside the village. In Japanese, a foreigner is literally called *soto no hito* or *gaijin* ("outside person"). In this case, if we take Japan to be *uchi* ("inside"), then foreign countries must be seen as *soto* ("outside").

To reduce the risk of dealing with the complications of relationships, the Japanese have traditionally tended to only really open up to share information and personal feelings with people whom they felt were *uchi* ("inside") their social circle.

In order to be welcomed "inside" (*uchi*), it is necessary that two persons know each other well both publicly and privately. Then they will be in a position where they can open up to their feelings (*jō*) as persons "inside" the same social circle and freely share information.

□ しがらみ barrier, complicated relationships
□ 心を許して let one's guard down
□ 捉える to consider
□ ある程度 to some extent

□ 〜に他ならない must be
□ 齟齬 contradiction
□ 軋轢 friction
□ のみ only
□ 〜する傾向にある to tend to

Feelings | *97*

日本人がビジネスの関係においても、よく夕食を共にし、お酒を飲んで騒いだりする背景には、お互いに「内」の関係になろうとする意識が働いているのです。これは、外国人のように日本社会の「内」に入りにくい人にとっては、常にお客さんとして扱われ、親切にはされるものの、打ち解けることができないという問題に直面するリスクもあるのです。

　日本で、「内」に迎えられるためには、まずビジネスライクな付き合いをやめて、プライベートな話を共有し、一緒に過ごす時間を増やしてゆく努力が必要なのかもしれません。

In terms of business, it is common for Japanese to have dinner and drinks together as they attempt to build a relationship in which they can both be "inside." For foreigners, who may find it difficult to break into the social circle, there is the risk that they will continue to be treated politely as guests without being able to get their Japanese counterparts to open up to them.

In order to be welcomed "inside" in Japan, it is necessary to not have a purely "business-like" relationship and instead to be sure to increase the time spent in sharing private interests.

☐ 意識が働く to attenpt to do
☐ 〜ではあるものの although
☐ 打ち解ける to open up
☐ 直面する to confront
☐ 共有する to share

本音と建前

「内」と「外」との関係を最も象徴的に表した言葉が、「本音」と「建前」です。「本音」とは、「内」の同じグループのメンバー同士で語られる本当に思っている内容のことで、「建前」は、**表向きの、**あるいは外交的なメッセージや言葉を指す表現となります。

日本人ならではのコミュニケーションスタイルを理解している人同士であれば、「本音」と「建前」とを**見分ける**ことは比較的簡単かもしれません。しかし、外国から来た人は、「建前」を聞いて、それを「本音」と勘違いし、あとになって**思うように事が進まず**にびっくりすることも**しょっちゅう**あります。残念なことに、この「本音」と「建前」を理解していない人から見れば、**あたかも日本人が嘘をついている**ように誤解することもあるかもしれません。

日本人から「本音」のメッセージを受け取るには、「内」に入ること、あるいは相手の属する「内」に**加わる人を通して**間接的に情報をとることが求められます。そして、何よりも、そうした**人を介して**相手を夕食などに招待し、お酒を酌み交わしながら、打ち解けてゆくことも大切です。

「本音」と「建前」は、外国の人にとって、**最もやっかいな**日本人のコミュニケーションスタイルのひとつなのです。

True Feelings and Facade

Two words that most closely represent the relationship of *uchi* ("inside") and *soto* ("outside") are *honne* and *tatemae*. *Honne* refers to the true feelings that are spoken by those who are "inside" (*uchi*) the same group, while *tatemae* is what is spoken for show or to be diplomatic.

For those who understand the Japanese communication style, it is relatively easy to see the difference between what is *honne* and what is *tatemae*. However, it is quite common for non-Japanese people to hear what is *tatemae* and misunderstand it as *honne*, later being surprised when things don't progress as they had thought they would. Unfortunately for those who cannot tell the difference between *honne* and *tatemae*, misunderstandings may sometimes arise where it is felt that the Japanese are not telling the truth.

In order to get the true intent (*honne*) of a Japanese person, one will be expected to become a member of his "inside" (*uchi*) group or go through someone who is inside the group. Above all else, it is then important to take that person out to dinner and have a few drinks with him in order to get him to fully open up.

For the foreigner, understanding *honne* and *tatemae* may be one of the most challenging aspects of the Japanese communication style.

□ 表向きの for show
□ ～ならではの special to
□ 見分ける to see the difference
□ 思うように as one had thought one would
□ しょっちゅう quite common

□ あたかも it is felt
□ ～を通して［介して］ through ~
□ やっかいな challenging

Feelings | *101*

7
忠
ちゅう
Loyalty

前章の「恩」の概念を思い出してください。

人から「恩」を受けると、**それに対する「義理」**が発生します。

「忠」は、その「義理」の中でも特に身分や立場の高い人に対して発生する義務を示す言葉です。

「恩」を与えてくれた人に対して、しっかりと敬意を表し、行動をもってその人に対して尽くしてゆく考え方が「忠」です。したがって、「忠」という概念は、より身分の上下がはっきりしていた封建時代において特に強調された道徳的規範であり、そこから派生する行動規範となるのです。

現代社会において、「忠」という意識をそのまま強要されることは少なくなりました。しかし、会社に対して忠誠心を持ち、時には自らを犠牲にしても会社のために労苦を惜しまず仕事をするという美学が、今でも日本社会には残っています。「忠」という意識は、日本人の心の奥深くに刻まれている遺伝子のようなものなのかもしれません。

Loyalty

Please recall our discussion of *on* ("debt" or "favor") in the last chapter.

One receives *on* from someone, and in turn one incurs *giri* (an "obligation").

Within the concept of *giri, chū* is the particular type of obligation that is incurred to someone of high rank or position.

The concept of *chū* means respecting and serving a person from whom one has received *on*. In the feudal period, when rank and position were even more clearly defined, the ethical norms of *chū* were therefore all the more emphasized.

In today's modern society, the awareness per se of *chū* is not as strong as it once was. However, even today in Japan, people will have loyalty to their company and from time to time sacrifice themselves by taking on undesirable assignments for the greater good of the company. It may be that this sense of *chū* ("loyalty") is grafted deeply into the DNA of the Japanese.

□ それに対して in turn
□ 尽くしてゆく to serve
□ 派生する to derive
□ 労苦を惜しまず painstakingly
□ 刻む to etch

□ 〜のようなもの kind of

Loyalty | *105*

上下

「上」と「下」の概念は、「忠」と大変深く関わっています。

今はもちろん存在しませんが、封建時代には、身分の「上下」が社会制度の基本でした。特に士農工商という４つの身分に人は分けられ、武士が最も高く、商人は最も低い地位にありました。そしてたとえば武士の中でも、幾層にも身分が分かれていたのです。

この身分の「上下」という考え方は、現代社会では、たとえば上司と部下、先生と生徒の間でみられます。あるいは生け花や茶道の学習にみられる家元制度などに強く受け継がれています。産業によっては、官と民間の間にも、大企業とその下請けの間にも、上下の意識が歴然と残っています。

日本では、相手の人格が自らより「上」の立場にあるか、「下」にあるかによって、言葉遣いも変われば、応対も違ってきます。

もちろん、欧米でも立場の「上下」はあり、相手がどういう立場かによって、ある程度は応対を変える習慣はあります。しかし、人と人とは基本的に平等で、挨拶の方法にそれほどの変化があるわけではありません。

しかし、日本では「上下」関係の「義理」に縛られた行動様式が、欧米よりも際立っていることは否めないようです。

もちろん、法律的にも制度の上でも、「上下」による差別は日本でも違法行為です。しかし、「上下」に関する人の意識は法的な規制とは別に、日本社会の根本原理として維持されているのです。

Hierarchy

The concept of "higher" rank and "lower" rank strongly influences *chū* ("loyalty").

During the feudal period, there was a strict system of hierarchy, although such a class system does not of course exist today. At that time, society was split into four classes: samurai, farmer, craftsman, and merchant, with the samurai at the top and the merchant at the bottom. Within the samurai class, there were several additional distinctions of rank.

In Japan today, *jōge* can still be seen in the relationship between boss and subordinate, or between teacher and student. It is also still very much alive in the disciplines of flower arrangement and the tea ceremony, for example. Depending on the industry, there may be *jōge* relationships in place between government agencies and private companies; and clearly a *jōge* relationship can be seen between large companies and their subcontractors.

In Japan, one's language and the way one interacts with another person will differ depending on whether the other person is "higher" or "lower" than oneself. For Westerners as well, the concept of "hierarchy" exists and the way one person greets another will differ to some degree depending on the status of the other person. In principle, however, people are treated as equals, and there is not as large a difference.

In Japan, however, it cannot be denied that the concept of *jōge* plays a greater role than it does in the West, due to the way in which *giri* ("obligation") strongly affects actions.

Of course, in Japan as well today, discrimination based on *jōge* is against the law. That said, the concept of *jōge* is still deeply rooted in Japanese society.

- □ 幾層にも several additional
- □ 家元制度 hereditary system
- □ 官と民間 government agencies and private companies
- □ 歴然と clearly
- □ それほどの (〜ではない) not as large
- □ 際立っている outstanding
- □ 否めない it cannot be denied

Loyalty | *107*

奉公

封建時代に「恩」を受けた人に**期待される**行動が「奉公」でした。

この「恩」と「奉公」との関係は、単にビジネスライクなものではありません。侍は、その一生、さらにその祖先から子孫へと、君主や上司から「恩」を受け、それに対する「義理」として「奉公」するわけですから、その紐帯は深く、単なる人間関係を超えた「情」と「義理」とで結ばれたものでした。

滅私奉公という言葉があります。その意味するところは、私情に左右されず、「恩」を受けた人に対して**とことん仕える**という倫理観を示しています。時には、自らの命を捧げて君主を守り、その行為に対して君主は、その人物の家族や子孫へも**さらなる**利益を与えてゆくのです。こうしてこの滅私奉公という、ある意味自己犠牲の考え方は**正当化**されるのです。

滅私奉公をすることによって、人は「恩」を与える者に対する「情」の深さを示し、その「情」によって気持ちを動かされた上に立つ者は、さらに「奉公」する者に愛情を注ぐのです。

このプロセスの**名残**が、現代社会にもあります。個人の予定よりも会社や上司のニーズを優先して残業をする意識など、一見過去の価値観と思われ**がちな**「奉公」という意識が、現在の日本人にも受け継がれ、大切な価値観となっていることには驚かされます。

忠 ちゅう

Service

During the feudal period, it was expected that *on* ("social debt") would be repaid through *hōkō* ("service").

This relationship of *on* and *hōkō* was not simply a business arrangement. For a samurai, the *on* that was incurred extended throughout his own life and stretched back to his grandfather and forward to his grandchildren, resulting in a deep bond with his lord that was based on *jō* ("feelings") and *giri* ("obligation").

Messhi hōkō ("self-sacrificing service"), is an expression that means to not be swayed by personal feelings in repaying through service the *on* that one has incurred. On occasion a samurai would have to give up his life in order to protect his lord, and in turn the lord would grant additional benefits to that samurai's family and descendants; in this way there would be compensation for the sacrifice (*messhi hōkō*) of the samurai.

Through one's service, a person shows the depth of his feelings (*jō*) towards the person to whom he has incurred *on* ("social debt"), and in turn that person will be further moved and show his affection for the person providing the service.

The product of this process continues to be found in Japan today. To a surprising degree, the values of *hōkō,* which had been thought to be old and passé, have continued on—in the way a Japanese will work overtime to put the needs of his boss or the company before his personal ambitions, for example.

□ 期待される expected
□ 滅私奉公 self-sacrificing service
□ とことん thoroughly
□ さらなる additional
□ 正当化する to justify

□ 上に立つ者 superior
□ 名残 vestige
□ 〜がち propense

Loyalty | *109*

忠義

　武士の社会では「奉公」という概念を、特に「忠義」という考え方に結びつけていました。「忠義」は、武士が自らの主君に対して**命を**かけて「奉公」することを示す言葉です。

　「忠義」は「武士道」の**根本を貫く**ストイックな精神で、主君を守るために死の恐怖をも克服して忠誠を保つことを 侍 に要求している価値観です。

　したがって、武士は徹底的に「忠義」を尽すことが美徳とされ、そのために常に精神的な修養と、武道の稽古、学問の研鑽が求められていたのです。

　「奉公」の概念が、武士に限らずより一般的に、「恩」に報いるための行為を示しているのに対し、「忠義」は武士が「奉公」するための意識を表す言葉として、彼らの倫理的な核となった言葉です。

　忠臣蔵という日本人なら誰でも知っている物語があります。この物語 は、ある君主が恨みのある身分の高い人物に刀で切りかかり、傷つけたことからはじまります。君主がその人物に貶められていたという事実にも関わらず、徳川幕府は君主に切腹を申しつけます。その君主のために、配下の武士たちが浪人となって討ち入りを果たし、君主の敵 をとったという実話なのです。その後、配下の武士たちは全員切腹を命じられます。

　しかし、彼らは死の恐怖を乗り越えて、亡き主君のために働いたわけで、そうした彼らの行為は、まさに「忠義」を全うしたとして、人々に語り伝えられたのです。

　「忠義」は、日本人があこがれる精神的な美学であるともいえましょう。

110 　忠 ちゅう

Loyalty

In the society of the samurai, the concept of *hōkō* ("service") was closely related to the concept of *chūgi* ("loyalty"). In other words, *chūgi* meant putting one's life on the line in service for one's lord.

Chūgi is at the root of everything to do with the samurai spirit; it is a basic value which requires the samurai to overcome the fear of death in order to maintain his loyalty to his lord.

It was expected that the samurai would do everything possible to maintain this virtue of loyalty, and that in order to do this he would constantly undertake spiritual, military, and scholarly training.

The term *hōkō* ("service") was used in a general way to refer to the service undertaken to repay *on* ("social debt"); in the case of the samurai, *chūgi* was at the ethical core of their *hōkō*.

There is a tale in Japan called *Chūshingura* with which all Japanese are familiar. Based on a true story, the tale begins with a certain lord pulling a sword at court and wounding a high official who had been maltreating him. Despite the fact that the lord had been responding to the bullying of the official, he is ordered to commit *seppuku* ("suicide") by Tokugawa shogunate. His retainers, who have become *rōnin* ("masterless samurai"), then carefully plan and execute the assassination of the official. For this, the *rōnin* themselves are ordered to commit *seppuku*.

This action on the part of the *rōnin*, overcoming their fear of certain death in order to revenge their deceased lord, has been passed down over the years as an example of what is precisely meant by *chūgi*.

Loyalty is a spiritual virtue highly prized by the Japanese.

□ 結びつける to relate
□ 命をかけて putting one's life
□ 根本を貫く fundamental
□ 核 core
□ 貶める to bully

□ 申しつける to order
□ 討ち入り assassination
□ 全うする to complete

孝

「目上」、「目下」という年齢差に起因する人間関係の中で、最も大切なものは親子の関係でした。

封建時代、武士は親子の間でも厳しい「上下」の隔たりがあり、父親は常に一家の長として、家族を監督する立場にあったのです。

そして、子供は「目上」である両親に対して敬意を表し、常に大切に遇してゆくことが、儒教道徳の上からも強く求められていました。当時、武士の子供は、両親に対してあたかも身分の異なる人に接するように、言葉遣いも変えていました。

この親に対する心構えを「孝」または「孝行」といいます。

「孝行」の発想は、日本のみならず他の多くの国にも見られ、とくに儒教道徳の影響の強い韓国で受け継がれています。

現在、親子の関係は以前とは比べものにならないほど、カジュアルになりました。「孝」に基づいた行動様式は、今ではほとんどみられません。

しかし、「孝行」という概念はよい価値観として、今なお教育の現場などでも取り上げられているのです。

112 忠 ちゅう

Filial Piety

Of all *me-ue* ("higher") and *me-shita* ("lower") relationships, the most important one is that between parent and child.

During the feudal period, there was a strict *jōge* ("hierarchy") maintained between parent and child, with the father at the top overseeing the entire family.

Under these Confucian morals, children were expected to respect their parents and always give them due consideration. At the time, children would speak to their parents as if they were persons of different rank.

This type of attitude towards one's parents was called *kō* or *kōkō* ("filial piety").

Filial piety is a concept that exists not just in Japan but in many other countries as well, including Korea, where the influence of Confucian morals is strong.

Compared to the past, the relationship today between parent and child has become much more casual. It is rare now to see actions being taken based on the principles of *kō*.

However, at schools and other places of learning, filial piety is still often used as an example of a strong social value that should continue to be respected.

□ ～に起因する be caused by
□ 隔たり distance
□ 遇する to treat
□ ～の上から under
□ ～のみならず not just ~ but

□ 比べものにならないほど can't compare
□ ほとんど（ない） rare
□ 今なお still

Loyalty | *113*

しがらみ

目上、目下、先輩、後輩、そして親子など、日本社会を彩る様々な縦の構造は、ある意味とても複雑で、それに対応するコミュニケーションスタイルも多岐にわたります。

そんな複雑な人間関係を日本人は「しがらみ」と呼ぶのです。

「しがらみ」とは、元々水の流れを止める設備のことを意味します。これが、複雑な人間関係を表現する言葉となったのは、人間関係が生んだ様々な「義理」に縛られて人間の自由な行動が束縛されるからに他なりません。

したがって「しがらみ」という概念は、そのまま「義理」にも繋がり、そして社会での様々なモラルとも直結します。

「義理」と「人情」の狭間で苦しむ人とは、まさにこの社会の「しがらみ」に捉えられて苦しむ人のことを意味しているわけです。

日本人が、自らの人間関係のことを「しがらみ」と表現する背景には、長い歴史の中で培われた様々な常識や硬直した社会制度に、日本人そのものがとらわれていることを示していることになります。

しかし、同時に、「しがらみ」は、人が自らの勝手で行動するのではなく、相手の立場や気持ちを考えてどのように動くかを判断させる、大切な価値観でもあるのです。

Barriers

Japan's vertical society, with its highly varied types of relationships such as superior, subordirate, senior, junior, and parent & child and so on is quite complicated, and requires one to constantly make choices as to communication style. The Japanese call these types of complicated relationships *shigarami*.

The word *shigarami* originally refers to a device used to stop the flow of water. The word took on its broader meaning in the sense that a person's freedom to act was restricted by the *giri* ("obligations") that he would incur.

In this way, the concept of *shigarami* is connected to the concept of *giri* and to other ethical and moral considerations in society.

It would certainly be the case that a person dealing with the difficult conflict between *giri* ("obligation") and *ninjō* ("personal feelings") would be an example of a person caught in the *shigarami* of society.

The use of the word *shigarami* to refer to the difficulty of relationships reflects the common practices of this inflexible society, which have developed over a long period of time.

However, at the same time it must be said that *shigarami* is a positive social value since it prevents people from acting for selfish reasons and instead encourages them to carefully consider the position of others.

☐ ～を彩る with its highly ~
☐ 縦の構造 vertical structure
☐ 多岐にわたる make choices
☐ 直結する directly connect to
☐ 捉えられる to be caught

☐ 硬直する to become inflexible
☐ 自らの勝手で for selfish reasons

Loyalty | *115*

8 神
かみ
The Gods

神 (かみ)

　日本人にとっての「神」とは、多くの場合、日本古来の宗教である神道での様々な「神」を意味します。

　神道は、明治時代に天皇を中心とした近代国家を建設しようとしたときに、国教化され、天皇の権威を象徴する宗教として政治的に利用されたために、大きな誤解を与えてきた宗教でもありました。

　神道は、元来ヒンズー教と同じ多神教で、日本各地に育まれてきた多彩な宗教でした。神道の信奉者は、滝や岩、そして湖や大木など自然の中に「神」が宿ると考えていました。日本人は農耕生活を営むにあたって、その地域を象徴する木や岩の精霊に豊作を願いました。そして村々の安全を願うための宗教行為の集大成でもあったのです。

　実際、石や自然物を崇めたり、水で清めたりする宗教行為は、北から南までアジア全般でみることができます。日本人にとって、そうした自然を象徴する事物の神秘を崇め、その前で身や心を清めることが、大切な宗教上の行為だったのです。神道は、こうした目的のために山にこもって修行し、鍛錬する山岳信仰などをも育みます。

　キリスト教や仏教などと違い、偶像を信仰の対象とせず、常に自然と向かい合うことが神道の特徴で、唯一例外として「神」の象徴として自然を映し出す「鏡」などが崇拝されることがあるのです。

　この古代から伝わる神道の考え方が、後年に大陸から伝来した仏教と重なり、日本人独特の精神的価値観が育まれます。

The Gods

When Japanese refer to *kami*, they usually mean the gods of the Shintō religion, which has been in Japan since ancient times.

Due to the fact that Shintō was instituted as a state religion for political purposes at the time of the Meiji Reformation, using the prestige of the emperor as its symbolic head, this religion has sometimes been misunderstood.

At its roots, Shintō was a diffuse system of beliefs that developed over time in local areas throughout Japan and, like Hinduism, had multiple gods. The followers of Shintō believed that the power of these gods resided in waterfalls, rocks, lakes, large trees, and other objects of nature. As an agricultural society, the Japanese would pray for an abundant harvest to the spirits symbolized by these objects; these religious rites also became an opportunity to gather together to pray for the safety of these various villages.

From the north to the south throughout Asia, it is possible to find religions that worship rocks and other objects in nature and that perform purifying rites with water. For the Japanese, who worshipped the mystery symbolized by nature, purifying one's body and soul before these objects was an important religious rite. With this objective in mind, various types of ascetic training in the mountains developed.

Unlike Christianity or Buddhism, there is no worship of idols in Shintō, where the worshipper is always at one with nature; the only exception to this would be mirrors used to reflect the symbols of nature.

The native Shintō later mixed with elements of Buddhism from the Asian continent to create the unique spiritual values of the Japanese. This mixing of Shintō and Buddhist elements is a trait of religion in Japan, and

---

□ 象徴する to symbolize
□ 多彩な diffuse
□ 〜に神が宿る gods reside in
□ 営む to engage
□ 集大成 grand sum

□ 崇める to worship
□ 清める to purify
□ こもる to stay holed up
□ 向かい合う to face

仏教の修行の中に、神道的な身を清める発想が加わり、実際仏教の寺院に仏を崇める堂の横に、神道での「神」を祭る神社が置かれたりするのも、日本の宗教の特徴といえましょう。

キリスト教とは違い、日本人にとっての「神」とは、人が自らの罪や贖罪を意識して対峙する「神」ではなく、自らを取り巻く自然への敬意と、清らかな自然に向かい、自らをも清めてゆく考えの中で創造されたパワーなのです。

can be seen in such things as Shintō-like purifying in Buddhist training; it is also not uncommon to find a Shintō shrine right next to a Buddhist hall of worship.

Unlike Christianity, where people are expected to atone to a god for their sins, the appeal of Shintō for the Japanese is to be found in the respect paid to nature and, through being unified with the purity of nature, to in turn become pure oneself.

□ 祭る to enshrine
□ 贖罪 atone
□ 対峙する to confront
□ 取り巻く to surround

禊
みそぎ

　岩や大木など自然の造物に魂や神が宿るとする神道において、最も大切とされる行為が、そうした精霊に向かうにあたって身を清める行為です。

　この身を清める行為のことを「禊」といいます。特に、神道などで、神のそばに仕える者は、水などで身を清め、常に清潔にしておくことが求められました。

　この「禊」の行為が、その後様々な形で日本の伝統の中に残るようになります。たとえば、お祭りで体に水をかけたり、元旦に冷たい海に入って一年の無病息災を祈ったりといった行為が日本各地にみられます。さらに、今でも山岳信仰で、滝にあたって身を清める風習があることなど、例をあげればきりがありません。

　日本人は風呂が好きで、シャワーではなく、湯船につかる習慣があります。湯船につかった後で、改めて体を洗う風習は、こうした「禊」のしきたりにその原点があるのかもしれません。

　「禊」の行為は、単に体をきれいにして神に向かうだけではなく、行為を通して心の「穢れ」も清らかにしてゆくものと信じられています。

　昔の日本人にとって、日々の生活の中に区切りをつけて、心と体を清め、改めて神に向かう行為は、生きてゆく上での大切な「けじめ」でもありました。

　今も、神社にお参りをする前は、神社の入り口や前にある水場で手を洗い、口をゆすぎます。その後で、日本人は神に向かって商売や家庭の平安を祈願するのです。

神

Purification

The act of purifying oneself before rocks, trees, and other objects of nature where spirits and gods reside is considered to be very important.

Such an act of purification is called *misogi*. For those in particular who participate in the rites of Shintō, it is expected that they will purify themselves with water, always keeping themselves clean.

The act of *misogi* can be found in many different forms in the traditions of Japan. For example, throughout the country one can see people pouring water over themselves at various festivals; or one might see people jumping into cold ocean water on New Year's Day as they pray for good health in the coming year; or one might find people standing under a waterfall as part of spiritual training in the mountains. There are countless examples.

The Japanese preference for taking a bath instead of a shower—washing themselves outside the tub before getting in—may be related to this custom of *misogi*.

The act of *misogi* is not simply a matter of cleaning one's body; the Japanese also believe that this is a cleansing of the soul.

For the Japanese of old, it was important to mark the distinction between everyday life and the time one would spend before the gods by first properly purifying the body and soul. Even now, before entering a shrine to pray, one will wash one's hand and rinse out one's mouth. It is only after purifying himself that a Japanese will then pray to the gods for the welfare of his family or business.

☐ 〜とされる be considered to
☐ そばに仕える to serve
☐ 元旦 New Year's Day
☐ 無病息災 good health
☐ きりがない countless

☐ 穢れ uncleanness
☐ 区切りをつける to mark the distinction
☐ ゆすぐ to rinse out

The Gods | *123*

穢れ

「禊」と深く関わる概念が「穢れ」です。

「穢れ」とは、**心身ともに穢れた状態を示します**。神の前に立つとき、人は穢れのない状態でなければならず、そのために「禊」を行うのです。

純潔という言葉があります。これは世界の多くの国にある古典的な価値観であり、文化現象ですが、**処女であること**、また子供のように純粋であることへの美学が神道における「穢れ」という発想の対極にもあるのです。

実際、神道では子供には大人にない神的なパワーがあると信じられており、**婚姻するまでの女性が純潔である**ことは、封建時代の道徳律などとあいまって、昔は大切なことであったのです。

子供のように純真ではなく、処女のように純潔ではない状態が穢れた状態とされ、人々は大人になってからも、神社などでそうした「穢れ」を**払おう**としたのです。

「穢れ」とは、単に**見た目が汚い**ということを超えて、邪悪な心を持つことそのものを指す言葉として捉えられていたのです。

Defilement

A concept that is closely related to *misogi* ("purification") is *kegare* ("defilement").

Kegare refers to both the defilement of the body and the soul. One must be purified before standing in front of the gods in order to not present a defiled self.

Many countries have the traditional value of "purity" in their cultures. In Shintō, this concept of being pure in the way that a virgin girl or child is pure also exists.

In Shintō, it is believed that children have spiritual powers that adults do not, and traditionally, it was considered ethically important that a woman remain pure until her marriage.

For adults, who were no longer pure like children or virgins, they would try to rid themselves of their *kegare* at shrines or other places of worship.

Kegare was not simply a matter of being physically unclean; in looks; it also referred to the wickedness in a person's soul.

☐ 心身ともに both the body and the soul
☐ 純潔 purity
☐ 処女 virgin girl
☐ ～と対極にある antithetical to
☐ 婚姻する to marriage

☐ ～とあいまって combined with
☐ 払う to rid
☐ 見た目 looks

The Gods | *125*

願

日本人は一般的に神社で神に自分の実利的な願いが叶うようにお祈りをします。

たとえば、子供が試験に合格して、高校や大学に進学できるように祈る人もいます。商売が繁盛するようにとか、個々人によって様々な祈願をするのです。

こうしたお願いを、真剣に行うことを「願をかける」といいます。「願」とは、「禊」を行って自らを清め、時には自分の欲望を抑えて心から「穢れ」をはらい、神に対してお願いをする行為です。

たとえば、お酒の好きな人は、「願」をかけている間はお酒をやめるという行為で、自分のお酒への欲求を抑えたりするのが一般です。

神道を強く信奉し、山を歩き、滝にあたって自らを清める行為を通して、修行を続ける人が昔から日本にはいました。彼らは仏教の影響も受け、経を読みながら、「禊」を行い、心身を鍛えて悟りをひらけるようにと「願」をかけます。

そうした人たちからみた場合、「願」とは単なる利益を得るために「神」に祈るという行為を超えた、精神的な高みを求めるための真剣な行為で、その行為を通してこそ望みがかなえられるという考え方なのです。

そして、「願」をかけて神に祈る行為を日本人は「祈願する」といいます。祈願とは「祈り、そして願う」という意味の熟語です。

Request

It is common for the Japanese to pray to the gods at shrines for their wishes to come true.

For example, one might pray for a child to pass a test or get into a good high school or university; or one might pray for the prosperity of one's business. People pray for a variety of things.

When one wishes to make a particularly important request, the Japanese use the phrase *gan wo kakeru*. When making such a request, one will first purify oneself, ridding oneself of defilement and controlling one's desires, before praying to the gods.

For example, if a person is fond of alcohol, it is common for him to give it up while the request.

Since ancient times, fervent Japanese believers in Shintō purified themselves and strengthened their bodies and minds through walks in the mountains and standing under waterfalls and other training. Over time, these believers were also influenced by Buddhism, and in the Buddhist tradition, would read sutras and pray for enlightenment.

Gan is more than simply making requests of the gods; it is an attempt to improve one's spiritual being, and through that process, perhaps one's requests will be answered.

The Japanese also use the word *kigan* (literally, "pray request") when praying to the gods to answer requests.

☐ 実利的な utilitarian
☐ 繁盛する to prosper
☐ 願をかける to make a wish to a god
☐ 一般である common
☐ 滝にあたる to stand under waterfalls

☐ 悟りをひらく enlightenment
☐ 望みがかなえられる one's requests is answered

The Gods | *127*

大和魂

　第二次世界大戦中、日本人を**鼓舞するために盛んに語られた言葉**が、この「大和魂」という言葉です。

　大和とは、古代の日本を示す言葉で、戦争中には軍国主義に利用され、この「大和魂」を強要された多くの若者が、戦いで**命を落とし**てゆきました。

　元々、「大和魂」とは、神道に根ざした清らかさを根本に、自然と共にそこに宿る神々を大切にし、生活を整えてゆく精神を指す言葉でした。

　明治時代になり、神道が皇室の宗教として国家によって**統率**され、国粋主義と融合したとき、「大和魂」は日本人の強く優れた精神性を表現する言葉となり、**以降**この言葉は国家威信を強調するために使われるようになったのです。そして最終的には、「大和魂」に「忠義」や「滅私奉公」の価値観が**集約**され、日本が全体主義国家として戦争へと**傾斜**していったのも事実です。

　確かに、神道は日本独自の宗教です。しかし、その**ルーツ**をたどれば、アジア各地に残る自然信仰や、ヨーロッパの森林信仰などにも結びつく、世界的に共有できる宗教でもあったわけです。「大和魂」はそんな神道を大切にする日本人の精神を表す言葉だったのです。

Japanese Spirit

During the Second World War, the phrase *yamato damashii* ("Japanese spirit") was often used to inspire the Japanese people.

Yamato is the ancient name of Japan. During the war, this phrase was abused by the militarists, and many young men were sent to their deaths in the name of *yamato damashii*.

Originally, *yamato damashii* was deeply rooted in Shintō, and referred to the spirit a person developed in purifying himself while being at one with the gods who resided in nature.

In the Meiji Era, Shintō became a state religion with the emperor at its head, and combined with nationalism, *yamato damashii* came to mean the strong national spirit of the Japanese. Thereafter the phrase was used to enhance national pride. And then later, in the 1930's, *yamato damashii* was combined with the concepts of *chūgi* ("loyalty") and *messhi hōkō* ("self sacrificing service"), as the nation slid down the slippery slope to a totalitarian state and war.

Shintō is in fact a religion unique to Japan. However, if one traces the roots of Shintō, one can find much in common with other animistic religions in the rest of Asia, that as well as in Europe. *Yamato damashii* is a phrase that expresses the importance Japanese place on the spirit of Shintō.

☐ 鼓舞する to inspire
☐ 盛んに often
☐ 命を落とす to finish one's life
☐ 皇室 imperial family
☐ 統率する to command

☐ 以降 thereafter
☐ 集約する to combine
☐ 傾斜する to slide down
☐ ルーツをたどる to trace the roots

The Gods | *129*

9 仏
ほとけ
Buddhism

仏
（ほとけ）

　日本に仏教が伝わってきたのは7世紀の頃ではないかといわれています。

　以後、仏教は時には権力者と結びつきました。後になると、権力者と結び権威となった仏教を批判する僧が出てきて、新しい信仰が生まれました。以来、仏教は民衆に広く伝搬してゆき、多様な形で受け入れられていったのです。

　「仏」という概念も、初期の仏教のように仏陀その人と深く結びついたイメージから、様々な流派が発展してゆく過程で、より人の苦しみを救済する「神」のようなイメージに置き換えられていきました。

　また、それと共に、禅のように修行を通じて自らの中に「仏」を見いだすという内省的なものから、ひたすら念仏を唱え、そのことによって来世での救済を期待するというものまで、信仰の方法も多様に変化してきたのです。

　さらに、日本古来の神道とも融合して、共に信仰の対象となったのも日本の仏教の特徴といえそうです。

　神道には、来世に対するイメージが弱く、自然界に宿る様々な神を信仰し、そこからのご利益はむしろ現世に対するものでした。そんな日本人に来世観を与えたのが仏教なのです。

　もともとインドに生まれ、中国を通して日本に伝わってきた仏教ですが、現在我々が日本で目にする仏教のほとんどが、日本人独自の宗教観によって変化してきた、日本ならではの仏教となっている点は、興味深いことであるといえそうです。

Buddhism

It is said that Buddhism came to Japan in the seventh century.

At some point, Buddhism became tied to the power structure in Japan. Later there was criticism of that association from certain elements of the priesthood, and as a result of that, other sects came into being. Thereafter, over time, Buddhism was spread widely among the people, taking many forms.

While in its early period, Buddhism was more directly associated with the Buddha himself; in later times, as more sects developed, Buddhism was repositioned more closely in association with the "gods" as a belief to save people from their suffering.

Together with this development, Buddhism moved from being primarily a meditative discipline, such as Zen, in which one sought enlightenment, to a more diverse belief system, which also included many sects more centered on chanting as a way of finding salvation in the next world.

Buddhism also combined with the native religion of Japan, Shintō, to create Japan's unique form of Buddhism.

In Shintō, there is not a strong connection to an afterlife; rather, the belief is in the elements of nature and how those elements can benefit one in this life. It was Buddhism that encouraged a Japanese belief in the afterlife.

It is interesting to note that although Buddhism originated in India and came to Japan from China, the Buddhism we see in Japan today is primarily a product of the unique religious beliefs of the Japanese.

□ 〜といわれている it is said that
□ 以来 thereafter
□ 多様な形で受け入れる to take many forms
□ Aその人 A himself [herself]
□ 仏を見いだす to seek enlightenment

□ ひたすら entirely
□ 唱える to chant
□ 目にする to see

自力と他力

禅のように、自らが行う修行を通して信仰を深めてゆこうという考え方を「自力」といいます。

それに対して、ただひたすら念仏を唱えることによって、来世での救済が約束されているというのが「他力」という考え方です。

「他力」の発想は、より多くの人を救済しようとする大乗仏教の流れによるものといわれています。

特に平安時代には阿弥陀信仰が広まり、貧困や病苦、そして戦乱に苦しむ民衆へと受け入れられてゆきました。念仏を唱えれば、阿弥陀仏によって死後、極楽に迎えられるという考え方で、この信仰を抱く人々の輪は、16世紀には大衆運動へと発展し、為政者をも脅かしてきたのです。

一方、禅宗のように「自力」を重んじる考え方は、武士などの支配階級に拡大してゆきます。

このようにして、「自力」と「他力」という二つの発想は、日本の風土の中で、「自力」の禅と「他力」の浄土宗、あるいは浄土真宗として育っていったのです。

現在でも「自力」、そして「他力」という言葉はよく用いられます。「人に頼らず、仕事は自力で開拓しなければ」といったように、宗教とは離れた次元で、こうした言葉が使用されているのです。

134 | 仏 ほとけ

Self-power and Other-power

Seeking through self-discipline, as in Zen, to deepen one's beliefs is known as *jiriki* ("self-power").

In contrast to this, seeking one's salvation in the afterlife through chanting to the Amida Buddha is known as *tariki* ("other-power").

It is said that *tariki* came from the grass roots movement of Mahayana Buddhism to save more people.

Particularly during the Heian Period in Japan, the creed of Amida spread, as the common poor and sick and those affected by war found its message of salvation through chanting appealing. In the 16th century, the number of people embracing these beliefs grew to the point that they became a threat to the ruling class.

On the other hand, sects like Zen, with its emphasis on *jiriki,* became popular with the samurai ruling class.

In this way, the primary sects of Buddhism in Japan developed: the Zen of *jiriki* and the Jōdoshū and Jōdoshinshū of *tariki*.

Even now, the words *jiriki* and *tariki* are often used in conversation. For example: "Rather than asking someone else, one must do the work on one's own (*jiriki*)." In phrases like this, we can see how these words are used apart from their religious origins.

□ 信仰を深める to deepen one's beliefs
□ 流れ movement
□ 念仏を唱える to chant appealing
□ この信仰を抱く to embrace these beliefs
□ 拡大する to become popular

□ 離れた次元で apart from

Buddhism | *135*

あの世

　仏教での死後の世界、**すなわち来世のこと**を、人々は**俗語**で「あの世」といいます。「因果」の項目でも解説しますが（第10章）、人はこの世での行いをよくすれば、「あの世」では極楽にゆくことができ、またよき人として生まれ変わるとされています。

　仏教が時代とともに日本で変化し、哲学としての仏教から信仰としての仏教へと変化する中で、この「あの世」の発想が大きく強調されてきました。

　それが、前項で紹介した「他力」の考え方と関係しながら、浄土宗、浄土真宗、そして日蓮宗といった新しい宗教運動へと発展し、**現代に至っているのです。**

　「あの世」が**あるということ**は、人々が現世で苦しんだり失敗したりする上での保証であり、救いであるといえましょう。そして、「あの世」があるということは、人に魂があり、死後も霊魂となってその人が存在することを意味します。

　それが、日本での葬儀やその後の死者を弔う様々な儀式へと発展していったのです。

　日本でよく語られる怪談話の特徴は、そうした霊魂が現世に対する恨みや執着が強く、「あの世」に旅立てず、幽霊となって現れるというテーマです。

136　仏 ほとけ

The Other World

The world after death in Buddhism, or in other words, the afterlife, is called *ano yo* ("the other world") in colloquial speech. In the section on *inga* ("cause and effect") in Chapter 10, we will discuss how people who conduct themselves well in this world will go to paradise in "the other world" and then be reborn in favorable circumstances.

As Buddhism changed with the times in Japan and developed from a philosophy into a religion, this concept of "the other world" was emphasized more. As noted in the last section, this development was related to the concept of *tariki* and led to the founding of the Jōdoshū, Jōdoshinshū, and then later the Nichiren sects.

It may be said that the existence of "the other world" acts almost as an insurance policy for salvation for those who suffer or fail in this world. In "the other world," a person continues to exist as a spirit after his death in this world.

That spirit is honored in Japan in funerals and other ceremonies held after a person's death.

There are many ghost stories in Japan about spirits who continue to be bitter and obsessed with this world and are not able to go on to "the other world."

□ すなわち in other words
□ 俗語 colloquial speech
□ 行いをよくする to conduct oneself well
□ 生まれ変わる to be reborn
□ 現代に至って down to the present day

□ ～があるということ the existence of ～
□ ～する上での upon
□ 弔う to mourn

Buddhism | *137*

たとえば、理不尽に殺された人が、殺人者の前に恨みをもって幽霊として現れるわけですが、その殺人者が処罰されたり、幽霊に悩まされて自殺したりした場合、幽霊となった霊魂は、安心して「あの世」に旅立ちます。

　そのことを俗語では「成仏する」というのです。すなわち、恨みや執着を捨てて、やっと「仏」の境地になって「あの世」、すなわち極楽に旅立ったというわけです。

138　仏 ほとけ

For example, a person who was murdered may go on to "the other world" only after the murderer has been executed or been haunted into committing suicide.

Going to "the other world" is called *jōbutsu* ("becoming a Buddha") in common speech. In other words, when a person is finally able to rid himself of the bitterness and obsessions of this world, then he is able to go to "the other world" of the Buddha, which is paradise.

□ 理不尽に unreasoningly
□ 処罰する to execute
□ 捨てる to rid
□ やっと finally
□ 〜の境地になる to go to 〜

Buddhism | *139*

もののあわれ

　仏教は、人の死を見つめる宗教でもあります。したがって、そこには儚い人生へのセンチメンタリズムが含まれています。

　元来、仏教は、人や宇宙の移り行く姿を捉え、自らの欲望を抑えて自然な姿に心を戻してゆく自省的な宗教であり、哲学でした。

　それが日本に伝来し、中世の矛盾の多い現世にあって、人々が来世に救いを求めるセンチメンタリズムへと変化してゆきました。

　たとえば桜は、春、ほんの数日間花を咲かせ、あっという間に散ってしまいます。この移ろいの中に美学を見いだしたのが、「もののあわれ」という美意識です。

　人も、いつ死を迎えるか予想できません。特に昔は、子供でも大人でも、あっけなく「あの世」に旅立ちます。それは桜と同じように哀れなもので、人の儚い人生に「もののあわれ」という美学を見出したのです。

　平安時代以降、「もののあわれ」という発想は文芸作品などに多くみられるようになりました。それが仏教での「他力」の発想と影響を与え合い、より宗教的な情緒へと変わっていったのです。

　「もののあわれ」は、日本人の美意識の奥にあって、現在でも多くの人が感じるセンチメンタリズムです。

　人は儚い存在であるがゆえに、お互いにその悲しみを癒し合うことは、「情」の価値観にも通じるものといえましょう。

140 　仏ほとけ

Pathos

In facing death and dealing with the fleetingness of life, an element of sentimentalism has developed in Japanese Buddhism.

In its origins, Buddhism was a religion and philosophy that dealt with the changing circumstances of humans and the universe, as people sought to return to their natural selves through self-reflection and the control of desires.

However, when Buddhism came to Japan and was faced with the conflicting realities of the middle ages, it evolved to meet the needs of those looking for salvation in the next world, and became more sentimental as it did so.

Cherry blossoms are one example. They bloom for only a few days in early spring before being blown off the trees. The sad beauty seen in this transition is what is meant by *mono no aware*.

No one knows when he will die. Particularly in the olden days, it was common to die suddenly at any age. As with the sad beauty of the brief life of the cherry blossoms, so it is with the *mono no aware* of the brief life of humans.

Starting in the Heian Period, one can see many examples of *mono no aware* in works of literature and art. The Buddhist concept of *tariki* ("other power") also came to influence *mono no aware*, giving it a more religious feeling.

Mono no aware is a form of sentimentalism deeply imbued in the Japanese sense of beauty.

It is necessary for people to support each other in overcoming the sadness of this fleeting life, and in that one will also find the concept of *jō* ("feelings").

□ 見つめる to face
□ 儚い fleetingness
□ 移り行く changing
□ ほんの only a few
□ あっという間に instantly
□ 移ろい transition
□ 見いだす to find out
□ あっけなく easily
□ ～であるがゆえに because of

Buddhism *141*

無常

　「もののの哀れ」が美学的な発想であるとするならば、それを仏教の視点からみた概念が「無常」という考え方です。

　すべてのものは常に変化し、生まれた者は必ず死ぬ。そして栄華もいつか必ず衰退し、常に同じ状態を保つものはこの世にはないというのが、「無常」の考え方です。

　ある意味で、これは仏教において仏陀が最初に抱いた悲しみであり、「無常」を感じることから、仏陀が涅槃にいたる足跡がはじまります。日本では、そこに「もののの哀れ」で示したセンチメンタリズムが付加されていったのです。

　中世の叙事詩として有名な『平家物語』は、琵琶を奏でる法師によって全国に広められました。「諸行無常」という言葉が、その叙事詩の冒頭に語られています。これは「無常」という概念をより具体的に示した言葉で、この叙事詩では平家という12世紀後半に栄華を極めた一族が、ライバルの源氏に滅ぼされてゆく様子が語られています。「栄える者もかならず滅びる」と、叙事詩では語っているのです。

　そして仏教の宗派の中には、「無常」であるが故に、阿弥陀仏を拝み、ひたすら念仏を唱えることで、苦しみのない来世へと迎えられると説く「他力」の宗派が生まれたのです。

Transience

If one considers *mono no aware* ("pathos") to be an aesthetic way of looking at things, then the Buddhist equivalent would be *mujō*.

All things are constantly changing, and all living things will eventually die. All that is glorious will decay, and there is nothing that will be able to maintain its current form—that is the concept of *mujō*.

In a certain sense, this was the first sorrow that Buddha embraced, and it was from this point that he began his journey towards Nirvana.

The sentimentalism of *mono no aware* ("pathos") was added to *mujō* when in Japan.

In the Middle Ages, the epic *The Tale of the Heike* was spread throughout Japan by monks who sang while playing the *biwa* ("Japanese lute"). At the beginning of the tale, it is stated that "everything is ephemeral, nothing is constant." This is a concrete example of *mujō*, as the story tells of the decline of the once all-powerful Heike at the hands of their chief rivals, the Genji. "The prosperous will always fall" is one of the themes of the story.

Then, in order to deal with the transience and pain of this life, sects centered around *tariki* ("other power") developed, using earnest chanting to the Amida Buddha to bring peace and salvation in the next life.

□ 視点 perspective
□ 無常 transience
□ いつか必ず one day surely
□ 涅槃 Nirvana
□ 足跡がはじまる to take a first step

□ 奏でる to play
□ 冒頭 beginning
□ 後半 last half

Buddhism | *143*

悟り

「諸行無常」を理解し、物事が起こり、変化する連鎖を見つめ、その連鎖の原因となる憎しみや欲望を**絶つ**ことによって、仏陀の境地へと至ることを「悟り」といいます。

「他力」を唱える宗派では、ただひたすら念仏を唱えることで、阿弥陀仏が**降り**てきて人々を引き上げてくれると信じます。

逆に、「自力」を唱える宗派では、様々な修行や瞑想を繰り返し、仏の心を体得しようと試みます。

天台宗の本山である比叡山には、千日回峰行という荒行があります。行者は1000日にわたり比叡山や京都を毎日30キロから多いときは80キロ歩いて巡ります。そして700日目にある堂入りでは、堂の中で7日半飲まず食わず、眠らず、座らずの状態でお経を読み、毎晩谷底の水を汲んで堂内の不動明王に供えるという行をこなさなければなりません。

こうして行を終えた人は大阿闍梨と呼ばれ、京都御所にも土足で参内できる**特権**を**得る**ことができます。

「悟り」を開くというのは、仏教徒にとっての共通の願いであこがれかもしれません。

日本人の間にも、そのあこがれは静かに受け継がれ、今も多くの日本人の**心**の支えの一つとなっているようです。

144 | 仏 ほとけ

Enlightenment

Having understood that "everything is ephemeral, nothing is constant," one then seeks enlightenment (*satori*). To do so, one rids oneself of one's enmities or desires by identifying their source and breaking the chain of such shortcomings, thereby advancing to the land of the Buddha.

Followers of the *tariki* sects believe that through earnest chanting they will be able to induce Buddha to come down and take them back to paradise.

On the other hand, the followers of the *jiriki* sects believe that through self-discipline and meditation they will be able to find salvation.

At the head temple of the Tendai sect, Hieizan, there is a rigorous regimen of training called *sennichi kaihōgyō* ("circling the mountains for one thousand days"). Over a thousand-day period, the supplicant walks between 30 and 80 kilometers a day around the Hieizan and Kyoto areas. Starting on the 700th day, there is a special period of seven-and-a-half-days during which the supplicant must read the sutras while not drinking, eating, sleeping, or sitting; each night he must also go down to the bottom of the valley to fetch water as an offering to the *Fudō Myōō*.

Those who complete this rigorous training are called *daiajari*, and as a reward, they are allowed to walk inside the Kyoto Imperial Palace with their shoes on.

For the followers of Buddhism, a desire to find *satori* ("enlightenment") is something they all have in common.

In Japan as well, the concept of *satori* has been quietly accepted and today is an important source of solace for many Japanese.

☐ 絶つ to rid
☐ 降りてくる to come down
☐ 本山 head temple
☐ ～にわたる extend over
☐ 土足で with one's shoes on

☐ 参内する walk inside the Imperial Palace
☐ 特権を得る to gain a privilege
☐ 心の支え spiritual support

禅

　日本の「禅」は、海外で最も広く受け入れられた仏教の宗派の一つといえましょう。

　鎌倉時代に中国から日本に伝わったとされる「禅」は、公案と呼ばれる師匠と弟子との問答を中心に修行をする臨済宗と、ひたすら座禅をする曹洞宗を中心に、全国に広がりました。

　座禅という瞑想を繰り返しながら、自らを見つめ、そこに「仏」に通じる仏性を見いだそうとする「禅」の行為は、「仏」と対峙するというよりも、瞑想を通して自らと向き合う宗教として、日本では特に精神鍛錬を日課とした武士階級に支持されてきました。

　「禅」は、日本文化にも様々な影響を与えてきました。

　質素で簡潔な生活習慣をよしとする「禅」の考え方に基づいて造られる禅寺にはじまり、そこでの作庭術や、茶道のたしなみ、さらには武術や武士の生活規範に至るまで、「禅」の影響をみることができます。

　ある意味で、今までみてきた日本人の価値観の中に、「禅」が見え隠れすることも否めません。たとえば、雄弁であるより寡黙であることをよしとする価値観や、自らの欲望を抑え、人に対応するコミュニケーションスタイルなども、「和」という日本人の基本的な価値観は、従来から日本にはあったにせよ、そこに「禅」の発想が加わることで、醸成されていったのではないでしょうか。

　禅宗が支配階級の道徳律の背骨として浸透してゆくなかで、宗派の違いを乗り越えて、禅的な発想法を日本人が好んで、自らの生活規範の中に取り込んできたのです。

146　仏 ほとけ

Zen

The Japanese sect of *Zen* is one of the most widely accepted forms of Buddhism in the West.

Imported from China during the Kamakura Era, *Zen* spread rapidly throughout Japan through the efforts of two sects: the Rinzai, which emphasized the question-and-answer approach between teacher and disciple known as *kōan;* and the Sōtō, which emphasized the meditative approach known as *zazen.*

Zazen's meditation places more weight on self-discovery than it does on intercourse with the Buddha, and in Japan this meditation became part of the daily routine of self-discipline and spiritual training for many in the samurai class.

Zen has also influenced Japanese culture in many different ways.

Starting with the temples themselves, which reflect *Zen's* emphasis on simplicity, the influence of *Zen* can be seen in such things as gardens, the tea ceremony, and the martial arts.

In a certain sense, it cannot be denied that *Zen* is present in some way in all of the Japanese values we have discussed to this point. For example, in the way that silence is valued over talking, or in the way that one's own desires should be controlled, or in the way that people communicate with each other—in all these ways we can see how the basic native value of *wa* ("harmony") was developed in tandem with *Zen.*

Zen permeated the ethical value system of the ruling classes, eventually transcending the sect to become an integral part of everyday life in Japan.

□ 見いだす to find out
□ 自らと向き合う to reflect on oneself
□ たしなみ etiquette
□ 見え隠れする be hidden in the background
□ 従来から heretofore

□ 〜にせよ even though
□ 背骨 backbone

Buddhism | *147*

煩悩

人間が持つ様々な欲望のことを仏教では「煩悩」と呼びます。

物欲、性欲、食欲、権勢欲など、煩悩には108種類あるといわれています。

除夜の鐘という儀式が日本にあります。大晦日に寺院が108回鐘を鳴らして、この「煩悩」を清めようとするのです。

仏教では、常にこうした「煩悩」をどのように克服し、「悟り」へと至るのかが課題となります。

仏陀自身、長い間瞑想を続ける中で、自らを苛む煩悩と戦い、最終的にそれを克服して「悟り」の境地、すなわち涅槃に至ったといわれています。

涅槃の状態を「寂静」と呼ぶように、それは「煩悩」によって心が騒ぐ状態を脱した、何もない静かな状態を指しています。

日本では、静けさを静寂という言葉で現しますが、それもこの「寂静」からきている熟語です。

日本人は「煩悩」という言葉をよく使い、「いやいや煩悩が多くてね」といえば、心配事や何かへの執着があって困っていることを示します。

そんなとき、日本人はふとお寺巡りをしに京都に行ったり、人によっては四国八十八箇所というお寺巡りの巡礼をしたりしながら、自分を見つめ直そうと試みるのです。

148 仏 ほとけ

Worldly Desires

In Buddhism, the various desires that humans have are called *bonnō*.

It is said that there are 108 desires, including desire for wealth, sex, drink, power, and so on. In Japan there is a ceremony called *joya no kane* ("New Year's Eve bell") in which the temple bell is rung 108 times on the final night of the year in order to cleanse away the 108 desires.

In Buddhism, one must constantly overcome desire in one's attempt to reach enlightenment.

It is said that the Buddha himself meditated for a long period, battling with his own desires before finally overcoming them and finding enlightenment, or in other words, reaching Nirvana.

The state of Nirvana is called *jakujō*, and as its Chinese characters suggest, it means reaching a state of nothingness and quiet, having rid oneself of desires.

In Japanese, the word *seijaku,* which is an inversion of the characters for *jakujō,* is used to mean "tranquility" or "silence."

The Japanese often use the word *bonnō* in everyday conversation. They might say, for example, "I have so many desires (*bonnō*)." In this case, it means that they have worries or obsessions that are troubling them.

When faced with a situation like that, a Japanese will seek to right himself through self-reflection, perhaps worshipping at temples in Kyoto or making the rounds of the 88 temples in Shikoku.

☐ 課題となる to become a issue
☐ 苛む to torment
☐ 克服する to overcome
☐ 脱する to rid oneself
☐ 熟語 phrase

☐ いやいや oh, no
☐ ふと casually
☐ 見つめ直す to reconsider

Buddhism | *149*

空
くう

　空気の項で、「空」という漢字の意味するところはすでに説明していますが、ここでは、仏教における「空」とはなにかを見つめたいと思います。

　「空」とは、何もない状態、からっぽの状態を示します。「空」は、「虚空」という熟語によって、非常に小さな状態を示す言葉にもなります。それは、**自我を限りなく小さくし、捨てる**ことにより、自らの中に**仏性**を見いだそうとする仏教の根本的な考え方に通じる概念なのです。

　「虚空」というきわめて小さい単位から、さらに無限に近く縮小してゆくと、そこに涅槃寂静という最小の単位に**到達**します。これは東洋での実際の数字の単位であると**同時**に、仏教でいう静かに悟った状態をも示します。

　現代の物質文明では、生活を豊かにし、欲望を満たすことが肯定され、精神の自由は豊かさによって獲得できるものとされています。ここに記す「空」は、それとは全く逆を示し、欲望を深めれば深めるほど、**渇き**は増してゆくと説いています。

　日本も資本主義国で、人々は金銭欲や物欲に**体**ごとつかっています。そして、確かに高度に発展した現代社会の中で、人々は精神的な疲れや渇きを抱いているのも事実でしょう。

　そんな日本において、人々は心の奥底に、こうした「空」への渇望、そして美意識を今なお抱いています。

　禅寺の簡素な庭を見るとき、どことなく**安らぎを覚える**日本人は数多くいるはずです。

150 　仏 ほとけ

Emptiness

In the section on *kūki* ("air"), we touched on the meaning of the Chinese character for *kū*. Here we will focus on the Buddhist implications of the character.

Kū denotes a state of nothingness, of being completely empty. In Japanese the word *kokū* also means a state of nothingness, but implies nothingness in a very small sense. One is able to find one's Buddha nature by shrinking down and ridding oneself of one's ego, the source of worldly desires.

Going beyond the already extremely small size of *kokū,* one continues to shrink one's ego ad infinitum until one reaches the nothingness of Nirvana (*nehanjakujō*). While this same word is used in East Asia as a unit of mathematical measurement, it also denotes the state of tranquility one reaches in enlightenment.

In today's materialistic society, people try to find spiritual freedom through an affluent life and the satisfaction of their desires. *Kū*, on the other hand, is the complete opposite of this: the more one seeks to meet one's desires, the less fulfilled one will feel.

Japan is a capitalist country, and many people are able to meet most of their materialistic desires. It is also true that in this highly economically developed country, many people are spiritually exhausted.

Deep in their hearts, many of these same people would strongly like to experience the fulfillment and beauty of *kū*.

There are still many Japanese who can feel completely at ease when they experience the simplicity of a *Zen* garden.

□ 自我 one's ego
□ 限りなく extremely
□ 仏性 Buddha nature
□ 到達する to reach
□ 同時に simultaneously

□ 渇き desire
□ 体ごとつかる be up to one's neck in
□ どことなく somehow
□ 安らぎを覚える to feel at ease

Buddhism | *151*

「無」と「空」とは非常に似た概念です。

仏教では、絶対的なものは存在せず、全てに原因と結果があると説きます。したがって原因がなければ結果はなく、欲望がなければ、悩みは存在しなくなります。そうした因果関係を超えて、いっさい何も無い状態に自分をおくことが「悟り」である以上、「無」という考え方は、仏教の根本を示す概念といえそうです。この哲学的なものの見方は、実は日本人の行動様式にも大きな影響を与えてきました。

「無」に至る最初の入り口は、相対的、客観的に物事をみることです。

それは、自分からの発想のみではなく、相手が何を望んでいるかを知ることで、人と人との交わりから生まれる因果関係を理解することを意味します。

この発想は、「和」の原理を持つ日本人には受け入れやすいものでした。自らの欲求を抑え、相手の意図を尊重しようという行動原理と、「無」へのアプローチが日本人のコミュニケーションスタイルに相乗効果を生み出すのです。

これが、「遠慮」の価値観にも影響され、日本人独特の会話方法となりました。そして、これが自らのニーズをしっかりと伝えるべきとする欧米人との間の誤解を招くことも多いようです。

「無」とは、どこにも中心がない状態です。

すなわち、自分の欲求が中心ではなく、そこには必ず相手の望みという別の軸も存在しているわけです。

究極の「無」とは、そうした欲求自体のない静かな状態に自らをおくことで、人へも救いを与える平安な状態が成立するという理想とつながるのです。

Nothingness

Mu is very similar to the concept of *kū*.

In Buddhism, there are no absolutes, and all effects have causes. Because there is no effect if there is no cause, there are therefore no worries if there is no desire. Going beyond the relation of cause and effect to find enlightenment (*satori*) in nothingness (*mu*) is one of the basic concepts of Buddhism. This philosophy, this way of looking at things, has had a large influence on Japanese behavior.

The starting point for reaching *mu* is to look at things in a comparative and objective way. To do so, one must begin by taking the point of view of other people rather than one's own, and from there, one first understands the connection between cause and effect in human relations.

For the Japanese, who place such importance on *wa* ("harmony"), this is an easy concept to accept. In other words, the principle of controlling one's desires and respecting the intent of others meshes well with the concept of *mu* to achieve an effective communication style for the Japanese.

This is a conversation characteristic of the Japanese and reflects their sense of reserve (*enryo*). It seems that this reserved approach often leads to misunderstandings with Westerners, who tend to put their own needs first.

In the concept of *mu*, one has no center in oneself. In other words, the desires of others are always central, rather than one's own desires.

Taking oneself to the ultimate state of *mu* puts one in an ideal condition of tranquility, which in turn allows one to help others.

□ いっさい completely
□ 入り口 starting point
□ 〜のみではなく not just
□ 交わり relations
□ 因果関係 connection between cause and effect
□ 誤解を招く to lead to misunderstandings
□ どこにも (〜ない) nowhere

Buddhism | 153

10
縁
えん
Relationships

縁

「縁」とは、人と人との出会いや離別からできる人間関係、そしてそこで培われるつながりを指す言葉です。

「縁」とは仏教で使われる言葉でもあり、仏によって結びつけられる人と人との関係を意味します。

「袖触れ合うも他生の縁」という言葉が日本にはあり、それは、ちょっとした出会いでも大切にしなければという意味を含んでいます。相手に敬意を払い、相手と最大限の「和」を保ってゆくことが、「縁」が求める理想です。

残念ながら、そうした考え方は、現代のビジネス文化の中では廃れつつあります。しかし、日本人が今なお、深い人間関係を求めようとしている傾向があることも事実です。ビジネスでも、お互いによく知り合うために食事やお酒を共にしたり、時にはプライベートな質問をしたりする背景には、こうした「縁」を大切にしようという伝統があるのです。

また、「縁」には人の力ではどうしようもない定めが作用していると仏教では教えます。

昔から、人に良くすれば、それは必ず自分の未来、また遠い将来生まれ変わった自分に返ってくるという発想があり、過去、あるいは前世の所行によって導かれる人との出会いや関係が「縁」という言葉で表されるのです。

「縁」は、人との関係を大切にしなければならないという、仏教によって生み出された倫理であり、道徳的な概念ともいえるのです。

Relationships

En describes the concept of a relationship, from first meeting to farewell, and the bond that is developed therein.

En is also a word used in Buddhism, meaning the relationships that are created by the Buddha as he brings one person together with another.

There is a phrase in Japanese that "even a chance encounter is preordained." This means that all relationships are important and must be taken good care of. The ideal is to treat each person with respect and make the utmost effort to maintain *wa* ("harmony").

Unfortunately, in today's global business culture, there seems to be a trend towards treating relationships as less important. However, it is a fact that the Japanese continue to place a great deal of importance on relationships. Even in business, the tradition of *en* remains alive as people get to know each other better by eating and drinking together, and on occasion, asking personal questions as well.

It is taught in Buddhism that one cannot change the *en* in one's life. This concept is called *sadame*.

Since olden times in Japan, there is the belief that if a person treats others well, that that good will return to him in the future of this life or in a life yet to come. The relationships that a person has formed through one's acts in the past of this life or an earlier life are called *en*.

En is a moral concept, grown out of Buddhist ethics, which emphasizes the importance of human relationships.

☐ 袖触れ合う their kimono sleeves touch each other
☐ ちょっとした trivial
☐ 〜つつある to be a trend towards
☐ 人の力 human power

☐ どうしようもない unavoidable
☐ 良くする to treat others well
☐ 所行 acts

Relationships | *157*

輪廻

　生きるものは全て宇宙の定め、そして「仏」の定めに従って、様々な生き物に生まれ変わり、生死を繰り返してゆくという考え方が「輪廻」の考え方です。

　仏教のふるさとであるインドなどでも、この考え方は古くから人々に影響を与えてきました。そして、「輪廻」という概念は仏教の伝来と共に、日本にも深く根をおろしたのです。

　「輪廻」とは過去から未来へとつながる生命の流れであり、来世でも幸福な人間として生を受けられるようにという、期待を人々の間に育みました。

　現在の日本では、この考えをそのまま信じている人はほとんどいないでしょう。

　しかし、日本人に来世観がなくなったかといえば、そうではありません。人は死後も魂となって、子孫のもとに現れ、時には子孫を守ってゆくものと漠然と期待する日本人は今でも多いはずです。

　また、現世で良い行いをすれば、それはどこかで必ず報われるはずだという期待は、今でも多くの日本人の心の奥底にあるはずです。

　日本に、死者を敬い、その魂を大切にしようとするためのお祭りや、仏教行事が多くあるのも、こうした「輪廻」や仏縁という考え方と無関係ではないのです。

158　縁 えん

Reincarnation

In *rinne,* all living things follow the laws of the universe and the Buddha, being born into this world in one form, dying, and then being reborn in another form in a never-ending cycle.

In the home of Buddhism, India, this way of thinking has influenced people since ancient times. Later on Buddhism brought the concept of *rinne* to Japan, where it also became deeply rooted in the society.

Rinne is the transition of life that links the past with the future, giving each person the hope that he will be happy in his next life.

In present-day Japan, there may be few people who believe in *rinne* per se.

That said, it is not true that the Japanese do not believe in a future life. There are many Japanese who continue to hold a vague belief that one's spirit is present after death and that that spirit remains near one's descendants, protecting them at times.

Deep in the hearts of many Japanese is also the expectation that good deeds done in this life will be rewarded in a future life.

The concepts of *rinne* and *butsuen* ("Buddha's fate") can also be seen in festivals and Buddhist ceremonies where the dead are honored and their spirits treated with importance.

□ 生きるもの all living things
□ ふるさと home
□ 根をおろす to take root
□ 生を受ける to come into the world
□ そのまま per se

□ もと nearby
□ 漠然と vaguely

Relationships | *159*

因果

「因果」はあらゆるものには原因があり、それによって結果が定められるという仏教の考え方です。

そして、「因果」は、「因果応報」という熟語で頻繁に使われる概念です。

仏縁の項目で説明したように、仏教には前世の悪行や善行によって人の運命が定められるという運命論があり、前世が原因であれば、現在の運命はその結果ということになり、それが「因果」という考え方となっているのです。

「因果応報」とは、単に前世と現在との関係にとどまらず、一生の間でも、自らがなした事柄は必ず自分に返ってくるという教えに基づいた言葉です。たとえば、若い頃に親不孝をして、その後自分が親になったときに自らの子供に苦しめられることがあったとすれば、それは典型的な「因果応報」となります。

また、罪を犯して逃げられたとしても、後に重い病にかかって苦しみ死んでゆくケースがあったとすれば、それも「因果応報」です。

「因果応報」は、いま自らを見舞っている災難や苦しみには、必ずその原因が存在するという考え方なのです。

原因と結果とを示す「因果」という考え方は、「仏縁」や「輪廻」という考え方とも関連し、「縁」という価値観を支える大切な概念となっているのです。

160　縁 えん

Cause and Effect

Inga expresses the Buddhist belief that for every cause there is an effect.

Related to *inga* is the often used phrase of *inga ōhō* ("as a man sows, so shall he reap").

As we saw in the last chapter on *rinne* ("reincarnation"), the good or bad that a person does in a past life will determine his fate in his next life; in other words, the causes of the last life will result in the effects of the next. This is *inga*.

The phrase *inga ōhō* is not limited to the cause and effect of one's past life on the present; one's deeds in this life will also come back to affect one's fate in this life. For example, if one does not take proper care of one's parents, then one may not receive proper care from one's own children. This would be a classic case of *inga ōhō*.

Another case of *inga ōhō* would be someone committing a crime and escaping, but later becoming seriously ill and dying.

In the concept of *inga ōhō*, it is believed that there is always an earlier cause for the difficulties or pains that one may be suffering now.

It may be said that *inga* is closely related to the concepts of *butsuen* ("Buddha's fate") and *rinne* ("reincarnation"), and that it supports the broader social value of *en* ("relationship").

☐ あらゆる every
☐ 因果応報 retribution
☐ 〜にとどまらず not limited to
☐ なす to do
☐ 親不孝 lack of filial piety

☐ 〜とすれば if
☐ 見舞う to suffer

Relationships | *161*

11 信 しん Trust

信

「信」とは信ずることから生まれる固い絆や安定した関係を示す言葉です。

「信」という漢字を分解すれば、左の部分は「人」を意味し、右の部分は「言葉」を意味しています。すなわち、言葉によって約定された人と人との強い信頼関係が「信」となります。

信頼を築く方法は様々です。たとえばアメリカでは、信頼の証は、まっすぐに相手の目を見ることと固い握手でしょう。そうすることで、相手が何も隠さず、正直に話していると感じられるのです。

では日本での信頼の証はどうでしょうか。相手の目を強く見つめず、相手に配慮して婉曲にものをいい、時には本音をあえて喋らずに、「謙遜」して自らの望みや実力も誇示しないことが相手から信頼されるコツかもしれません。

こうしてみると、二つの異なった文化に生きる人同士では、同じ「信」の概念を大切にするにしても、その表現の仕方は正反対ということになります。これは、ある意味ではとても危険なことと言えましょう。

言葉さえ通じれば、人はみな同じという考え方がいかに深刻な誤解の原因になるかということは、この「信」という概念に対する行動様式の違いをみると明白です。

164　信 しん

Trust

Shin refers to a strong and stable bond established between two or more people.

If one breaks down the Chinese character for *shin*, one will see that the left side means "person," while the right side means "speak." In other words, the speech exchanged between people become the promises which result in a strong relationship of trust.

Trust may be gained in different ways. For example, Americans try to gain trust by looking directly into the other person's eyes and making a strong handshake. By doing this, it is felt that one is making his thoughts clear, without hiding anything.

In Japan, on the other hand, it may be said that trust is gained by being modest and not putting one's desires first, by being sensitive to the other person's position and speaking in an indirect manner as necessary, and by not looking into the other person's eyes in too aggressive a manner.

In this way, we can see that while both cultures have their own way of expressing trust, they are in fact completely the opposite of each other. This can be a dangerous thing.

It is clear from this discussion about *shin* how serious misunderstandings can occur by assuming that people are the same simply if they can speak each other's language.

☐ 固い絆 stable bond
☐ 約定する to promise
☐ 築く to build
☐ 婉曲に in an indirect manner
☐ コツ knack

☐ 正反対 completely the opposite
☐ 〜さえすれば as long as

Trust | *165*

仁
じん

「仁」という漢字を分解すると、左側が「人」、右側が「二」で、人が二人という意味になります。人が二人になったとき、お互いのことを意識し、相手にどのように対応するか考えます。つまり、そこに社会というものが生まれるのです。

「仁」とは、その人と人との接し方、社会での振る舞い方の知恵と愛情を示す言葉で、古代中国の儒教の根本概念を現す漢字として日本にも伝わりました。

古代、国を治めるには、社会においては「上」を敬い、「下」を慈しみ、家庭においては父母に「孝」を尽くし、隣人を大切にしてゆくような社会をつくることが必要とされました。「仁」は、そうした考えを示す言葉です。

儒教は、日本に伝来して以来、支配階級の規律や心得の哲学として取り入れられ、日本人の道徳律に大きな影響を与えてきました。特に江戸時代にその影響は強く、儒教の一派である朱子学が身分制度を維持する思想的背景として取り入れられ、徳川幕府の基本理念となりました。

166 ｜ 信 しん

Benevolence

If we break down the Chinese character for *jin*, we will see that the left side of *jin* is the character for "person," while the right side is the character for "two." When two people get together, each is aware of the other person and must consider how to deal with that person. In other words, this is where this phenomenon we call "society" begins.

The concept of *jin* came to Japan from China early on as one of the basic tenets of Confucianism, denoting this interaction between people as knowledge and love are exchanged.

In ancient times, in order to maintain stability throughout the country, those above oneself were respected, those below were cherished, in the home filial piety was observed with one's parents, and one took good care of one's neighbors. *Jin* reflects the values inherent in these actions.

After arriving in Japan, Confucianism became an important part of the moral code and philosophy of the ruling class, and subsequently came to have a large influence over the ethics of all Japanese. This influence was particularly strong during the Edo Period, when the teachings of the Shushi school of Confucianism were used to support the strict class system of the Tokugawa government.

☐ 知恵　knowledge
☐ 国を治める　to govern a country
☐ 慈しむ　to cherish
☐ 尽くす　to use up
☐ 心得　understanding

「仁」をしっかりと心得、実践する人が「信」に足る、すなわち「信用」できる人として尊敬されたのです。

儒教の始祖である孔子の言葉をまとめた論語に、「巧言令色、鮮なし仁」という有名な言葉があります。これは言葉が巧みで、愛想のよい表情をする人間ほど、思いやりや慈しみの心が少ないものだという意味の格言です。

この言葉からも理解できるように、日本人が寡黙であることを美徳とする背景には、儒教の影響も強くあるのです。

168 信 しん

Those who actually lived their lives in keeping with the practices of *jin* were respected as people who could be trusted.

There is a famous saying by Confucius: "The man of flowery speech knows little about benevolence." What this means is that the more skilled a person is in flowery speech, the less sincere he is in his heart about the needs and feelings of others.

These words reflect again the strong influence of Confucianism in the importance the Japanese ascribe to the virtue of taciturnity.

□ ～に足る be worthy of
□ 始祖 founder
□ 巧み skilled
□ 愛想のよい amiable
□ 格言 proverb

仁義

「仁」を実践するには、人と人との約束事、すなわち「義」を大切にしなければなりません。「義」とはすでに解説した「義理」に通じる考え方と思えばいいでしょう。

この二つの漢字を合わせると「仁義」となり、人と人との約束事をしっかりと守ることの大切さを説く熟語となるのです。

もちろん、「仁義」は武士などの支配階級では「忠義」という言葉に置き換えられ、大切な価値観として尊重されました。

そして、庶民レベルでは、友人との約束や、人から与えられた「恩」に対してありがたく思うことが、「仁義」と解釈されてきました。そういう意味で、「仁義」は、やくざの世界などでは特に重んじられ、親分と子分との間の「仁義」をめぐる葛藤などは、今でも映画の題材として取り上げられています。

言い換えれば、「仁義」を守ることが「信」につながり、「信」を得るためには、「仁義」に厚い心を持つことが大切です。

「内」と意識した人間へは、その人を裏切らないように、「仁義」がうまれます。相手に対して「仁義」を感じることが、相手への「情」にもつながるのです。

170　信 しん

Moral Code

In order to be a person of benevolence (*jin*), one must honor one's *gi* ("commitments"). In this case, *gi* is the same Chinese character used in *giri* ("obligations"), which we discussed earlier, and the two words have the same basic meaning.

If we combine the characters for *jin* and *gi*, we get *jingi*, which, as we noted above, denotes the importance of honoring one's commitments.

Among the ruling classes, the word *chūgi* ("loyalty") could be substituted for *jingi*. *Chūgi* was of course a particularly important value for the ruling classes.

Among the common people, on the other hand, *jingi* was interpreted as the promises kept among friends or the *on* ("social debt") that had been incurred with someone. *Jingi* in this sense is an especially important value for the yakuza, and there are even now many movies made where the central theme is complications in the commitments between a yakuza boss and his underling.

Putting it another way, honoring one's moral code (*jingi*) engenders trust (*shin*), and in turn trust strengthens one's commitment to one's moral code.

In order to not betray those who are in one's inner circle (*uchi*), one must have *jingi*. Having a sense of *jingi* means that one also has a sense of affection (*jō*) for those with whom one interacts.

□ 義 commitment, justice
□ 置き換える to substitute
□ 庶民 common people
□ ありがたく思う to appreciate
□ 解釈する to interpret

□ やくざ Japanese Mafia
□ 厚い cordial

Trust | *171*

12 徳
とく
Virtue

徳

「徳」とは、日本人の価値観に精通し、それを実践し、そのことによって世の中にも必要とされる知性を指します。

したがって、「徳」のある人とは、人から尊敬され、何か必要なことがあれば、その人の意見を求め、時にはその人に**教えを請い**ます。

では、「徳」のある人物とはどのような人物像でしょうか。

まず、**なんといってもその人は**「謙譲」の精神をもって、常に控えめで、自分をアピールすることなど**決してありません**。腰が低く、「情」と「義理」とをよく理解しています。

その人は、しかも「道」を極めた「匠」かもしれません。しかし、すでに世の中の**酸いも甘いも知り尽くし**、厳しさよりも、穏やかさをもって人を包み込むような人かもしれません。

「徳」のある人は、人生の達人で、決して**堅物**ではありません。礼儀作法をしっかりと**嗜み**、道徳をよく心得ながらも、楽しむことにかけても達人です。日本人の知恵や価値観を集約した知恵。それが「徳」の意味するところなのです。

174　徳 とく

Virtue

The principle of *toku* ("virtue") is known and practiced by the Japanese, and through *toku* one learns what is necessary to be wise.

People of virtue are respected, and when necessary, a person will seek out their opinion or ask that they serve as a teacher.

What type of a person would we describe as being virtuous?

First, such a person is *kenjō* ("modest"), never seeking to blindly promote his own interests. He also has a good understanding of *jō* ("feelings") and *giri* ("obligation").

Furthermore, such a person may have the *takumi* ("skill") to "take the road (*michi*) as far as it will go." But it is also true that such a person may have already reached a point where he is confident and settled, and is neither bitter nor naive about life.

A virtuous person has mastered life, and knows how to adjust to its twists and turns. He is also a master of being able to enjoy life, following proper etiquette with grace while maintaining an ethical spirit. Being able to integrate wisdom with principle—this is the definition of *toku*.

□ 教えを請う to ask someone for instruction
□ なんといっても after all
□ 決してありえません never
□ 腰が低い humble

□ 酸いも甘いも知り尽くす to taste the sweets and bitters of life
□ 堅物 too serious person
□ 嗜む be fond of

名

「名」とは、人の表の顔です。元々「名」は人の名前のことで、その人にとって最も大切なアイデンティティとなります。

そして「名」は、その人にとっての名誉、そして地位をも意味します。社会的にしっかりとした地位を築いたとき、人はあの人は「名を成した」といいます。そして一般的に「名」を成した人は、「徳」をも備えていることが期待されます。

「名」を成すということは、出世し人々から尊敬される人のことですから、そのことによって、その人は、外見上は少なくとも名誉を勝ち得たことになります。そのような人にとって名誉を維持することはとても重要です。名誉とは、精神的に高潔であることと、社会的に認められことの二つの側面を持ちますが、時にはその二つは矛盾することもあります。武士にとっては、精神的に高潔であることが本当の名誉とされていたのですが、現実はというと、やはり人間は弱い者で、表面上の社会的地位を維持することによって、「名」を維持してきた人が多いようです。

「名」を維持することが、もし、何らかの理由で困難になったとき、その名は「恥」で汚されることになります。

176 徳 とく

Name

Na ("name") is the outward representation of a person's face. The root meaning of *na* is "name," an essential aspect of a person's identity.

Na also refers to a person's honor and position. When a person has built a solid position for himself in society, that person is said to have "established a name" (*na wo nashita*). It is expected that such a person will be virtuous.

A person who has established his name (*na*) is respected by people, meaning that, at least for outward appearances, he has earned a certain degree of honor and prestige. For such a person, it is very important that he maintain his honor. There are two aspects to honor: the internal integrity that one maintains and the external recognition that comes from society. Sometimes these two aspects of honor can be in conflict with each other. For the samurai, internal integrity was supposed to be the true definition of honor, but being human, it seems that in many cases, the external recognition of society was just as important, if not more so.

Maintaining one's *na* becomes difficult if, for some reason, one stains one's name with *haji* ("shame").

- ☐ 名を成す to establish one's name
- ☐ 備える to equip
- ☐ 出世する to rise in life
- ☐ 少なくとも at least
- ☐ 高潔 integrity

- ☐ 側面 aspect
- ☐ 現実はというと in real life
- ☐ 何らかの理由で for some reason
- ☐ 汚す to stain

Virtue

恥
(はじ)

「名」は「恥」と表裏一体の価値観です。

「恥」とは、単に恥ずかしいことではなく、自らが大切にする「名」を汚すことによって損なわれる名誉心を意味する言葉です。

欧米の人は、キリスト教的な倫理観にそぐわない行為をしたときに、「罪」の意識を感じるといわれています。それに対して日本人は、「罪」ではなく「恥」の意識を抱くわけです。

「恥」とは、内省的に自らに問いかけて恥ずかしく思う他に、共同体の他の人々に対して恥ずかしく思うという意識もついてきます。常に他とのバランスの中で、自らが特に過ちなどを犯して特異な状況になることに対して、人は「恥」の意識をもつのです。

たとえば、死を畏れて戦いから逃げてしまった武士がいるとして、その武士は自らの弱い心を見つめて恥じ入るのと同時に、家族や同僚や同郷の人々、そして自らが仕える君主に対して「恥」の念を持ちます。

また、儒教的な観点からは、先祖に対して恥ずかしく思うといったように、祖先、時には子孫への「恥」という多面的な意識を抱くのです。

確かに、「和」を重んずるせいか、日本人は自らが行動するとき、常に他人のことを気にする傾向にあります。他人と異なる行動をするとき、多かれ少なかれ日本人は「恥」の意識と戦わなければならず、それを克服して自らの意思を通してゆくための勇気が要求されるのです。

Shame

Haji ("shame") is the opposite side of *na* ("name").

Haji is not simply doing something embarrassing; it means staining one's name and thereby losing one's honor.

It is said that Westerners will view an act that is contrary to the ethics of their Christian moral law as a sin. Rather than sin, the Japanese are concerned with *haji* ("shame").

As well as an introspective questioning of oneself, the concept of *haji* also involves how one is viewed by the surrounding community. One must always maintain one's balance with others, seeking to avoid making a mistake that will put one at odds with the community and result in *haji*.

For example, if during a battle a soldier were to desert his unit out of fear, he would not only have to come to terms with himself about his shameful act, he would also have to deal with the *haji* he had brought on his family, his comrades, his country, and if he were a samurai, the lord he was serving.

As in Confucian thought, the concept of avoiding *haji* extends to one's grandparents and can also include one's grandchildren.

Most likely due to the importance placed on maintaining *wa* ("harmony"), the Japanese tend to always be concerned about what others will think. Whenever the Japanese do something different from what most other people would do, even if it is not significantly different, they must find the courage to battle and overcome their feelings of *haji*.

☐ 損なう to lose
☐ 過ちを犯す to make a mistake
☐ 特異な abnormal
☐ 恥じ入る to feel ashamed
☐ 念 feeling

☐ 気にする to worry about
☐ 意思を通す to stuck to one's will

Virtue | *179*

面目

　よく中国人は面子を大切にするといいます。

　その人の立場を尊重し、その人の体裁を傷つけないようにすることを、中国の人は「その人の面子を守る」といいます。

　日本にも面子の概念も「面目」という言葉も存在します。自らの名誉を大切にし、自らの名に恥じないよう気をつかってゆくことを、人は「面目を保つ」というのです。

　日本人は、「面目」が潰れたとき、「恥」を意識し、「面目」が潰れる原因をつくった人に対して怒りを覚えます。

　たとえば、会議で上司が自分の意見を言ったとき、部下がそれに反論すると、上司は「面目」を潰されます。ですから、部下は上司の体裁を保つために、その場では強く反論せずに、後で別の「場」をもって上司に自らの考えを伝えるのです。

　そうした意味で、「面目」という価値観は、「和」や「場」、そして「間」などの概念とも深く関連しているのです。

　人前で自らの意見を表明することを悪いこととは思わない欧米の価値観と、この「面目」という価値観は鋭く対立します。日本人にとって、「面目」とは相手の立場を考え、相手に「恥」をかかさないように「配慮」することの大切さを教える価値観です。

　相手の気持ちになって物事を考えれば、自然と「面目」は保たれ、人との「和」が維持できるのです。

Face

It is often said that the Chinese place a great deal of importance on "face."

In other words, the Chinese "save face" when a person's position is respected, and nothing is done which would harm that person's social standing.

The Japanese have a similar concept of "face" (*menboku* or *mentsu*). One must "protect one's face" (*menboku wo tamotsu*) by taking care of one's honor and ensuring that one's name is not stained with *haji* ("shame").

A Japanese person will feel shame if he loses face, and he will be angry with the person or people who have caused him such shame.

For example, if a person were to openly oppose his boss during a meeting, the boss would lose face. In order to avoid this, the subordinate in this case would seek a different *ba* ("place") to present his views to his boss.

In this sense, the concept of *menboku* is closely related to the concepts of *wa* ("harmony"), *ba* ("place"), and *ma* ("space").

The concept of *menboku* tends to conflict sharply with the norms of Westerners, for whom voicing one's opinion in front of others is not a bad thing. For the Japanese, on the other hand, it is important to always consider the position of others and ensure that no *haji* ("shame") is brought to them. If one keeps the feelings of others in mind, *menboku* ("face") will be saved without making any special efforts, and *wa* ("harmony") will be maintained.

- ☐ 面子 face
- ☐ 体裁 appearance
- ☐ 〜ないようにする to try not to
- ☐ 面目 face
- ☐ 気をつかって to take care
- ☐ 面目が潰れる to lose one's face
- ☐ 怒りを覚える to feel angry
- ☐ 鋭く sharply
- ☐ 恥をかかせる to put somebody to shame

Virtue | *181*

分
ぶん

「分」とは日本に古くからあるその人の立場にあった言動を期待する価値観です。昔は身分の低い者には身分に応じた「分」があり、たとえば身分の高い人の司る領域に口を挟み、意見をいうことはタブーでした。そうした行為は、「分をわきまえない行為」とされ、厳しく追及されたのです。

現在では「分」は、自らの社会的地位や会社での上下関係などの中に織り込まれた価値観となっています。

新入社員は自らの「分」を守って、「先輩」に敬意を表し、上司の指示に黙って従いながら、仕事を学びます。学校でのクラブ活動では、下級生は上級生が活動する場所を掃除し、言葉遣いも丁寧にし、それぞれの立場での「分」に従った練習することが期待されます。

この「分」を逸脱した行動をした場合、相手の「面目」を潰すことになるのです。

縦社会の典型のように思われるこの「分」という概念が、今なお日本人の心の中に生きていることには驚かされます。

全ての人は平等であると規定されている現代社会においての「分」という考え方。それは、お互いに摩擦なく相手を尊重して組織や社会の「和」を維持するための暗黙の了解とでもいえそうです。

Role

The principle of bun concerns the "role" that a person was expected to play based on his position in society. In the old days, it was taboo for a person of low rank to approach or talk to a person of high rank. This was known as *bun wo wakimaeru* ("understanding one's role"), and such practices were strictly enforced.

Today the principle of *bun* is still commonly found in the *jōge* ("hierarchy") relationships, which one maintains according to one's social position.

For a young person just joining a company, he will play his *bun* by respecting his *senpai* ("seniors") and obediently following their directions in learning his job. In clubs at school as well, it is expected that each person will play his *bun*, with the newer, more junior students using polite language towards the older, more senior students, while also doing chores such as cleaning up after them.

When a person does not properly play his *bun*, he may "do damage" to the "face" of another.

It is surprising that this concept of *bun*, which may be thought of as typical of a classical "vertical society," is still alive now in the hearts of Japanese.

In today's society, where all people are expected to be treated equally, it can be said that the implicit consent behind the concept of *bun* contributes to the overall *wa* ("harmony") maintained in companies and other organizations.

□ 司る to take charge of
□ 口を挟む to interrupt
□ 追求する to heckle
□ 織り込む to weave in
□ 新入社員 new employee

□ 面目を潰す to damage someone's honor
□ 摩擦なく without friction
□ 暗黙の了解 implicit consent

阿吽の呼吸

　ここに記してきた日本人の価値観に支えられた様々なコミュニケーションスタイルを使いこなすことによって、相手に敢えてすべてを語らなくても意思疎通ができる状態を「阿吽の呼吸」といいます。

　たとえば、相手の立場を理解して、自らの「分」をわきまえれば、口に出して説明しなくても、その「場」での言動はコントロールできます。

　「和」の精神が理解でき、「型」を心得ていれば、敢えて人に対してその行為について詳細を質問する必要もありません。

　すなわち、こうしたプロトコールがわかっていれば、言葉を少なくしても、相手に意思や意図を伝えることができるのです。

　言葉を交わさなくても、即座に相手の意図が理解でき、その期待に合致した行動がとれる間柄、すなわち「阿吽の呼吸」の間柄こそ、「内」の関係であり、本音で話せる親しい関係といえましょう。

　ある研究によると、日本人は欧米の人に比べて、言葉の行間の意味を理解し、より簡単に文脈で意思疎通ができるということです。しかし、この発想は、日本人同士の価値観に基づいた交流を理解できない欧米の人にとっては誤解の原因となります。

Intuitive Communication

For the Japanese, who with their shared social values are able to use a variety of methods to communicate, getting one's point across with a limited amount of words is known as *aun no kokyū* (literally, "breathing in harmony").

For example, if one understands the position of the person one is dealing with, and one is able to properly play one's *bun* ("role"), then one will be able to control the flow of the conversation of that particular setting and it will not be necessary to use many words.

If one understands the spirit of *wa* ("harmony") and the *kata* ("form") of the moment, it will not be necessary to ask detailed questions about what is happening.

In other words, if this type of "protocol" is followed, a person will be able to express his intent with a minimum of words.

It is precisely this type of relationship, where one is able to have one's intent immediately understood by the other person without the use of words, which the Japanese would describe as *aun no kokyū*.

Studies done in the past show that, compared to Westerners, the Japanese are able to fill in meanings based on context more easily. This can lead to misunderstanding on the part of Westerners who are unfamiliar with this type of communication used between Japanese.

□ 使いこなす to use thoughtfully
□ 分をわきまえる to know one's place
□ 言葉を交わす to exchange words
□ 合致する to correspond with
□ 行間の意味 hidden meaning between the lines
□ 文脈 context

Virtue

諦観

「分」という価値観を思い出してください。

昔から「分」は、身分や上下関係と深く関わった価値観として捉えられてきました。その発想で人間全体を一つのグループとして考えれば、その上にあるものとは神や仏、あるいは宇宙といった、**人知を超えた存在**であるということになります。

人間は人間である以上、こうした超越的な存在に対しても「分」を持ちます。たとえば、人は死を**超越**できません。また、**未来を見通す**ことや、過去を変えることもできません。

そんな人間の限界を人間の「分」として捉えることが、人間としての知恵をもった人、すなわち「徳」のある人ということになります。

「諦観」とは、そのまま訳せば「あきらめ」ということになりますが、実際は、何が人間の「分」であるかを心得ることを意味し、その**限界を知る**ことを「諦観」と呼んでいるのです。

従って、知恵ある人、「徳」のある人は、「諦観」を**併せ持っている**はずです。

人が新たなことにチャレンジすることはよいことであるとしながらも、人の存在そのものの限界を理解することによって、より人にやさしく接するというのが「諦観」の持つ美学なのです。

「礼」という価値を知ることによって、人の社会での知恵を抱き、「諦観」を抱くことによって、より大きな自然や宇宙、そして神や仏の存在に敬意を払うことが、「徳」を磨いた知恵者に求められる究極の条件であるといえるのです。

186　徳 とく

Resignation

Please recall our earlier discussion about the concept of *bun* ("role").

From ancient times, *bun* has been closely related to rank and *jōge* ("hierarchical") relationships. If we think of humans as one group, then in terms of *jōge*, the rank above humans would be a god or gods, space, or something else beyond human knowledge.

Humans also have a *bun* ("role") to play in relation to such a transcendent being. For example, humans cannot overcome death. Humans also cannot see the future or change the past.

People who understand these limits in a profound sense as the *bun* ("part") to be played by humans may be considered wise; in other words, they are persons of virtue (*toku*).

Taken literally, *teikan* means "resignation." However, what *teikan* truly means is the wisdom of understanding human limitations and discovering what one's *bun* ("role") should be within those limitations.

It follows that wise and virtuous people will also understand the true meaning of *teikan*.

While it is a good thing to challenge new objectives, one of the virtues of *teikan* is a tendency to treat other people better, which may come from understandings our limitations.

To be recognized as a polished person of virtue and wisdom, the ultimate requirement may be that through our understanding of *rei* ("etiquette") and *teikan* ("resignation"), we pay the proper respect to our gods.

□ 分 role
□ 人知を超えた beyond human knowledge
□ 超越する to overcome
□ 未来を見通す to see the future
□ 限界を知る to understand one's limitation

□ 併せ持つ to have both
□ 〜としながらも while

Virtue | *187*

13 美
び
Beauty

日本の「美」とはどのようなものでしょうか。
　日本の「美」を語る上で、**際立った四季**があることは重要です。日本は温帯に**位置**するため、春夏秋冬、それぞれの季節感が際立っています。季節ごとの風物や美術や工芸、さらには日本料理があり、その季節ならではの**特長**が活かされているのです。
　また、日本人は季節の移ろいに、仏教での「無常」を重ね、儚い人生をそこに**投影**させてきました。日本の古典文学では、このテーマが常に繰り返されています。
　こうした季節感は、日本人を観念的なものより、むしろビジュアル的な表現方法へと**駆り立**てます。
　近世の絵画を代表する浮世絵や、現代の漫画やアニメまで、その**原点**をたどれば、四季折々の風物をただ写生するのではなく、デフォルメして**表現**してきた伝統に**到達**します。
　たとえば秋という季節感をいかにして**表現**するかは、山野の風物をそのまま描くより、紅葉を幾葉か組み合わせ、美しい線で描いた方がより**鮮明**に人々に**訴え**かけます。
　こうしたデフォルメによるミニマリズムは、古くは禅寺の石庭にはじまり、線と色の組み合わせのみで表現する浮世絵や、文芸の世界では短い語句の中に自然や事物への**思いを盛り込む**俳句などにみられる、日本の芸術の特徴といえましょう。

190　美び

Beauty

What exactly is beauty for the Japanese?

Among other things, it must be said that within the Japanese concept of beauty, the ebb and flow of the four seasons is very important. Geographically located in a temperate zone of the earth, Japan is a country where summer, fall, winter, and spring can all be experienced to their fullest. Each season has its own art, its own crafts, and certainly also its own food, each of which reflect the nuances of that particular time of the year.

For the Japanese, too, there is the Buddhist element of *mujō* ("transience"), which adds to the sense of impermanence seen in the changing of the seasons. This theme is a common one in classical Japanese literature.

The Japanese tend to express this sense of the seasons more visually than conceptually.

Rather than simply sketching the various elements of the four seasons as they appear directly to the eye, a tradition of expressing things in a more indirect manner has developed in modern wood block prints, manga, and anime.

For example, in depicting a fall scene, one may be able to make a deeper impact by drawing the fine lines of colorful leaves arranged in a pattern rather than a broader scene of mountains and fields.

It may be said that this type of indirect expression and the minimalism with which it is associated are particular features of Japanese art. Starting in ancient times with the gardens of Zen temples, these features can be seen in the lines and colors of wood block prints as well as in the abbreviated form of poetry known as *haiku*.

□ 際立った ebb and flow of
□ 位置する be located on
□ ～ごとの each
□ 投影させる to project
□ 駆り立てる to urge on

□ 原点をたどる to get back to the grass roots
□ 訴えかける to make an appeal
□ 思いを盛り込む to put some feeling into

わび

　色とりどりのきらびやかなものより、簡素でひなびたものの中に見いだす美しさを「わび」といいます。

　15世紀、「わび」は茶道などと共に語られるようになった美学で、それは茶器や茶室など目に見えるものだけではなく、無駄を排除し、質素なライフスタイルの中にやすらぎを見いだそうとする禅の発想とも融合して、人々の間に広がりました。

　たとえば、宝石をちりばめた器で美酒を飲むよりも、素焼きのお椀で清水を飲む方が、より味わいがあり、風雅であるというのが「わび」の考え方です。自然の中に自らをおいて、身の回りのものは最低限にし、季節の移ろいを肌で感じることに心の安らぎを得、同時に世の「無常」を思うことができるというのが「わび」の概念です。

　「わび」は、日本人が最も大切にする精神世界でもあり、物欲による贅沢ではなく、精神的な贅沢を求める上での理想であるともいえるのです。

The Beauty of the Simple

Wabi is the beauty found in the simple and desolate, as opposed to the beauty found in bright colors.

Wabi was a concept that began to emerge as part of the tea ceremony in the 15th century. Over time it spread across Japan not simply in reference to the simplicity of the tea house or the tools of tea, but more broadly in connection with the Zen philosophy of meditation.

For example, *wabi* would dictate that rather than drinking *sake* from a cup elaborately inlaid with jewels, it would be more refined to drink spring water from an unglazed bowl. *Wabi* might be felt, too, when one is alone, surrounded by nature, observing the changing of the seasons and also sensing the transience of this life.

Wabi is a very important aspect of the Japanese value system, where the ideal is found not in the luxury of things, but rather in the luxury of the spirit.

□ 色とりどりの very colorful
□ きらびやかな bright
□ ひなびた desolate
□ やすらぎ comfort
□ ちりばめる to inlay

□ 味わい taste
□ 肌で感じる to get the feel with one's skin

Beauty | *193*

さび

　「わび」と共に、時には対で語られるのが「さび」という概念です。「さび」とは、古くなり劣化したものの中に見いだす美の世界です。

　たとえば、古い日本家屋の廊下などは、時とともに磨かれ風化して木目が見えてきます。そんな家に住めば、夜、雨戸がガタガタと鳴ることによって、冬の前触れである木枯らしを実感し、その音をじっくり味わいながら俳句をつくるといったことが、「さび」であり、「わび、さび」と一つにして語られる美学なのです。

　また、日本の仏像は塗料がはげ落ちても、そのままにされ、現れた古木の美しさの中で微笑む仏像に人々は祈りを捧げます。朽ちてゆくものへの美意識がなければ、造られた当時の彩色を施し、新しく生まれ変わった仏像を安置するはずです。

　実は、質素で古いものをうまく使いこなし、そこから茶道や華道といった様式美が生みだされたことからも理解できるように、「わび」や「さび」の世界はそれを「美」の世界へと高めた洗練なのです。

　日本庭園では、よく苔が使われます。

　石を配置するとき、苔むした石を置くことで、「さび」の世界を表現しようとするのです。枯山水という庭園では、あえて池を造らず、石と砂と樹木で自然を表現し、石庭では樹木すらおかずに石と砂のみで自然界を表します。

　それは簡素で古くなったもの、つまり「わび、さび」の概念で造られるミニマリズムの世界なのです。

The Beauty of the Decaying

The concept of *sabi* is often spoken of together with the concept of *wabi*. *Sabi* is the beauty found in that which is old and decaying.

For example, one might see *sabi* in the worn grain of the polished wood of the corridors of an old Japanese house. And if one were to live in such a house, one might experience *sabi* (or both *wabi* and *sabi*) in hearing the sound of the night shutters being opened or closed, and hearing those sounds, one might recall the cold of the winter and be moved to write a *haiku* poem.

In Japan, people may be seen praying to old statues of the Buddha where the lacquer has fallen off and only the bare wood remains. If there were no such appreciation of the beauty of the decaying, then these old statues would be repainted and restored to their original state.

As can be seen in the tea ceremony and flower arrangement, *wabi* and *sabi* are not only the appreciation of the simple or the old; they also represent the refinement of such elements into the realm of "beauty."

Moss is commonly used in Japanese gardens.

Sabi is expressed by using moss-covered rocks in the garden. In the style of garden known as *karesansui*, no water is used, and nature is represented only with rocks, sand, and plants; in the style known as *sekitei*, only rocks and sand are used.

This is a minimalist world created with the simple and the old, or in other words, with *wabi* and *sabi*.

□ 対で in pairs
□ 劣化する to decay
□ 前触れ herald
□ じっくり thoroughly
□ 朽ちる to decay

□ 彩色を施す to paint
□ 苔むした moss-covered

Beauty | *195*

艶(つや)

　艶とは、洗練されていることを示す言葉です。
　「わび、さび」の概念からもわかるように、決して贅沢なものを着こなし、きらびやかなものの中に身を置くことが洗練ではありません。歴史的にみるならば、「わび、さび」は都会人の嗜みでした。こうした一見贅沢に見えないおしゃれな感覚は、そのまま時代とともに受け継がれ、庶民の美意識の中にも浸透していったのです。
　江戸時代に、都会ならではの遊女との享楽や色恋が浮世絵や当時の出版物で流布するようになると、おしゃれに遊ぶことが艶なことだとされ、町人の間で、様々なライフスタイルが流行します。
　特に、当時の為政者が質素倹約を法制化したこともあり、贅沢には様々な規制が押し付けられました。そうした中で、表には現れない贅沢さ、そしておしゃれが追求されたのです。元来派手好きな町人は、敢えて目に見えないところや、ちょっとしたアクセントに気を配り、贅沢を追求したのです。
　艶とは、「わび、さび」の概念を取り入れながらも、派手好きな町人の生命力が融合し、都会的な洗練へと進化した美意識であるといえましょう。
　江戸時代、「艶」のある人といえば、セクシーでおしゃれな人という意味で、庶民のあこがれとなっていたのです。

Refinement

The word *tsuya* means "refinement."

As was seen in our discussion of *wabi* and *sabi*, it is not considered refined to dress oneself up in luxurious and glittering clothing. From an historical point of view, we can see how *wabi* and *sabi* came to reflect the tastes of city people. Over time, this "non-luxurious" stylishness came to be a part of the sense of beauty held by the common people.

During the Edo era, what was *tsuya* ("refined") came to be influenced by what was going on in the licensed districts. Wood block prints (*ukiyoe*) of dandies with the women of these districts became popular, setting the tone for fashion and other aspects of the daily life of the townspeople.

At that time, the authorities had regulations in place to enforce a frugal lifestyle, and there were many restrictions on any ostentatious displays of wealth. Given these circumstances, the townspeople were forced to adopt more subtle expressions of luxury and fashion, using an accent here or there in their attire, or even in their under-clothing, which could not be seen.

It may be said that *tsuya* combined the concepts of *wabi* and *sabi* with the townspeople's innate love of the flashy to produce the big-city sense of beauty.

During the Edo era, a person who was refined was seen as someone who was fashionable and sexy.

□ 着こなす to dress oneself stylishly
□ 歴史的にみる to see from an historical point of view
□ おしゃれな stylish
□ 享楽 pleasure

□ 色恋 love affair
□ 流布する to prevail
□ 押し付ける to force to adopt
□ 表には現れない not be seen

Beauty | *197*

雅
みやび

京都は長い間日本の首都として、宮廷がおかれていました。その千年の歴史の中で培われてきた宮廷文化が醸し出す、優雅で洗練された雰囲気を「雅」といいます。

宮廷やそこに生きる貴族によって守られてきた「雅」な文化は、浮世絵などに代表される町人文化が醸し出す「艶」と対照的な美意識です。

15世紀後半から16世紀にかけて、日本は戦国時代となり、当時京都にあった幕府が衰退し、日本全国で大名という有力者が覇権を競い戦い合っていました。大名は自らの領国を豊かにするために、進んで京都の文化を取り入れます。その過程の中で「雅」が全国に広がっていったのです。

17世紀に、江戸（現在の東京）が日本の行政の中心になった後も、朝廷は京都にありました。江戸や大阪は当時の経済の中心として、躍動的な町人文化が栄え、それに押されるように京都の文化は衰退してゆきました。

しかし、「雅」という美意識はその後も受け継がれ、今では古都京都の美しさそのものを指すようにもなったのです。

そして、戦国時代以来、各地に広がった染物や陶磁器などの工芸に代表される京都の文化は、今なおそれぞれの地域で保存され、多くの人が地方に根付いた「雅」な伝統を守っているのです。

Elegance

As the capital of Japan, Kyoto was the location for the imperial court for a very long time.

Over that thousand-year history, the culture of the imperial court developed a graceful elegance which in Japanese is called *miyabi*.

The culture of *miyabi* developed by the nobles at the imperial court was in direct contrast to the culture of *tsuya* of the common people represented in wood block prints (*ukiyoe*).

During the latter half of the 15th century and into the 16th century, Japan went through a period of almost constant war. During that time, the central government in Kyoto went into decline, as the *daimyo* ("regional lords") came to dominate the politics of the country. In their quest for power, the *daimyo* sought also to bring into their own domains the culture of Kyoto, and it was through this process that *miyabi* spread throughout Japan.

Even after the central government moved to Edo (present day Tokyo) in the early 17th century, the imperial court remained in Kyoto. During this period, Edo and Osaka became the economic centers of Japan and the culture of the townspeople flourished, while that of Kyoto faded.

The sense of beauty found in *miyabi* did not disappear, however, and even now when one hears the word *miyabi* one thinks of the elegance of the culture of old Kyoto. After the wars of the 15th and 16th centuries, dyeing and pottery and other handicrafts of Kyoto spread throughout the country, and today they continue to be strongly rooted in the local communities.

☐ 醸し出す to create
☐ 雰囲気 atmosphere
☐ 覇権を競う to struggle for supremacy
☐ 進んで willingly
☐ 中心になる to play a key role
☐ 押されるように losing ground
☐ 古都 former capital

Beauty | *199*

儒教道徳の影響を強く受けた武士を除けば、日本人は一般的に性に対して開放的でした。「色」とは、絵の具の「色」という意味の他に、恋や性を示す言葉として、今なお使われています。

色恋沙汰といえばセックススキャンダルのことですが、江戸時代も、庶民は色恋沙汰が大好きで、それが当時の歌舞伎や文楽といった芸能の題材になり、浮世絵でも取り上げられました。

当時の幕府は、そうしたテーマを扱うことを規制しますが、人々はその網の目をかいくぐって逞しく創作活動を続けたのです。

「色」は「艶」にも通じ、都会人のお洒落なライススタイルとして支持された概念です。

たとえば、春画と呼ばれる浮世絵があります。これは、江戸時代のポルノといってもよく、男女の交わりの様子が克明に描かれたもので、今では貴重な絵画として日本のみならず、世界で高価な値段がつけられています。

江戸時代、庶民は奔放に「色」の世界を楽しんでいたのでしょう。

そして今でも、日本を訪れた外国の人は、日本の開けっぴろげな風俗産業の隆盛ぶりにびっくりするそうです。

実際、性に対するタブーの多いキリスト教やイスラム教の影響の少ない日本では、「色」という概念はそのまま人々に受け入れられ、性のテーマは漫画などでも頻繁に取り上げられています。

「色」は、日本人の美意識の一部として認知されているのです。

Erotic

Excluding the prudish Confucian attitudes of the samurai, the Japanese have in general tended to be open-minded about sex. In Japanese, *iro* refers not only to color but can also refer to love or sex.

The Japanese of the Edo era also liked their sex scandals, and these scandals were often used as the subject matter for the *kabuki* or *bunraku* (puppet) dramas.

The government at the time had regulations in place to restrict dramas using such themes, but loopholes were found and the production of these dramas continued to flourish.

Iro can also be seen as an element of being refined (*tsuya*), as part of the drinking and night-life culture of the big city.

For example, there are wood block prints (*ukiyoe*) known as *shunga*. These prints, essentially the pornography of the Edo era, today fetch high prices on world markets as precious examples of a unique form of Japanese art.

It seems that the common people enjoyed the world of *iro* without restraint during the Edo era.

When non-Japanese visit Japan, it seems that they are often surprised at the openness and prosperity of the country's "pleasure" industry.

Japan has little of the influence of Christianity or Islam and their taboos on subjects related to sex. Being more open-minded, it is common in Japan to take up themes related to sex in *manga* or other popular forms of entertainment.

For the Japanese, *iro* is seen as one aspect of their overall sense of beauty.

□ 開放的 open-minded
□ 網の目をかいくぐる to slip through the dragnet
□ 克明に in detail
□ 奔放に without restraint

□ 開けっぴろげな openly
□ ～ぶり way of doing

Beauty | *201*

粋（いき）

　粋とは、「色」や「艶」の世界を心得えて、人生を生きる人を表す言葉です。

　これはある意味で、江戸時代にあった都会的なダンディズムといえましょう。また、**気の利いた**気配りや、為政者の庶民の気持ちを理解した判断なども「粋」という言葉で表現されます。

　たとえば、母親の病気の薬を買う**お金ほしさに**盗賊の盗みの手伝いをした者がいたとして、江戸時代に司法長官であった町奉行がその者の罪を許して仕事を与えたとします。庶民はそれを「粋」な**はから**いといって喝采するのです。

　「粋」とは、小さなことでありながら、センスがよくアクセントの利いたことを示します。この事例の場合、町奉行が法制度を変革しようとすることは職務であって「粋」なことではありません。この**各論**でのかわいそうな犯人を救った小さな判断が「粋」なのです。

　同じように、たとえば部屋の中の小さな花瓶に椿をひと折り入れておいたとしましょう。それは大きな花の飾り付けではありませんが、訪れる人にちょっとした安らぎと季節感を与えます。それが「粋」なアレンジなのです。

　「粋」なことは決して雄弁であってはなりません。それは**ささやかで**、目にはつくものの、普段なら気づかないようなことにちょっとした工夫や**心遣い**が**施されて**いるものが「粋」なのです。

Chic

A person who is *iki* understands the worlds of *iro* and *tsuya*.

It may be said that *iki* represents the "dandyism" of the Edo era. *Iki* can also be expressed in the thoughtfulness of one person towards another, for example in how people in authority might understand the needs of the common people in making judgments.

Let's say that in the Edo era, a person helped out with a robbery in order to buy medicine for his sick mother, and the judge, rather than sending the guilty person to prison, arranged a job for him. This would be applauded by the common people as an act of *iki*.

While an act of *iki* is usually small in scale, it has good sense and a strong impact. In the example used here, the judge is not trying to bring about a major change in the law; he is simply trying to help one unfortunate person, and that is why this is a case of *iki*.

In the same way, let's say that we displayed a single camellia in a small vase. Even though this is a small display of a single flower, it gives people coming into the room a sense of peace, while also signaling the season. This would be an example of an *iki* arrangement.

When being *iki* it is not necessary to be eloquent. One can be *iki* by doing a small thing to bring attention to something that would usually not be noticed.

☐ 気の利いた thoughtful
☐ お金ほしさに for money
☐ はからい arrangement
☐ 各論 particular case
☐ ささやか small

☐ 工夫 device
☐ 心遣い consideration
☐ 施す to administer

Beauty | *203*

幽玄

「わび」や「さび」の概念で、飾り気の無い素朴なものや、古く朽ちたものをじっと鑑賞していると、そこに時を超えた不思議な奥深さを感じることがあります。その情緒を人々は「幽玄」と呼んでいるのです。

また、日のかげりや夕暮れ時に漂う不安定な闇など、自然界の微妙な移ろいの向こうに感じる宇宙の深淵にもつながる静寂も「幽玄」の意味するところです。

深遠なる静寂はまた「妖」なる世界でもあります。というのも、「わび」や「さび」は、永遠の時の流れの中で風化し、朽ちてゆくものへの愛着を語る言葉であり、それは「無常」の概念に従って、死にゆくことへの美学にもつながっているからです。

中世以降日本人に親しまれてきた伝統芸能である「能」は、まさにこうした美しさを追求した舞踏劇で、その多くに死者の霊魂が語る場面がもうけられています。

「幽玄」とは、日本人の抱く美意識の中でも、最も伝統的で洗練された美しさへの価値観であるといえましょう。

Profound Tranquility

As discussed in the sections on *wabi* and *sabi*, when one closely observes the old and decaying or that which is of extreme simplicity, one can be moved beyond time to feel a surprising profundity. This is called *yūgen*.

Yūgen may also be found in the uneasiness felt at the end of the day as darkness approaches, or in the subtle changes of the natural world as one looks into the tranquility and the abyss of space.

A profound tranquility is also part of the world of the bewitched (*yō*). In this same way, *wabi* and *sabi* are also connected to the aesthetic of death, as these sensibilities reflect the eternal passage of time and with it, decay and decline and the eventual transience to death.

The traditional Noh drama, a part of Japanese culture since the Middle Ages, places importance on this particular sense of beauty, often including scenes where the spirits of the dead speak of their trials.

It may be said that *yūgen* is a very traditional and refined aspect of the Japanese sense of beauty.

□ 飾り気の無い simple
□ 時を超えた beyond time
□ 奥深さ profundity
□ 情緒 emotion
□ かげり declining

□ 妖 bewitched
□ もうける to set up

Beauty

風流

　月見というイベントがあります。中秋の名月とは、澄んでひんやりとした秋の空気の中にみる満月の美しさを指す言葉で、そんな月を愛でることを月見というのです。こうした伝統的な美意識を体験することを、日本人は「風流」と表現します。

　この章に記した日本人の美意識をもって物事を鑑賞し、それを楽しむことが「風流」なことで、そうした行為を日本人は洗練されたものと感じるのです。

　「風流」を体得し、それを実践できる人は「風流人」と呼ばれ、文化人として尊敬を集めます。

　「風流」とは風の流れと書きますが、その表記の通り、風が流れるようにさりげなく、心地よく日本の伝統美を表現できる人こそが「風流人」であるといえるのです。

　そうした意味では「風流」は「粋」にも通じる概念で、それは日本人があこがれる感性であり、ライフスタイルです。

　もちろん、「風流」な人は美意識が洗練されているだけでなく、「徳」がある教養人となります。すなわち、日本人がよしとする価値観を体得し、それを美的なセンスをもって優雅に表現できる人が「風流」な人なのです。

206　美

Cultured

In the autumn there is an event called *tsukimi*. *Chūshū no meigetsu* refers to the beauty of a full moon viewed on a clear autumn night; it also refers to the event itself of admiring the moon in such fashion. The Japanese call the experience of appreciating such a sense of beauty *fūryū*.

Observing things with the Japanese sense of beauty, as described in this chapter, and enjoying that experience is *fūryū*. The Japanese consider such behavior to be very refined.

One who understands the true meaning of *fūryū* and who is able to put it into practice is called a *fūryūjin* and is respected as a person of culture.

The Chinese characters for *fūryū* mean "flow with the wind," and indeed a true *fūryūjin* is one who, like the movement of the wind, is able to express his appreciation of traditional Japanese beauty in a seemingly effortless way.

In this sense, *fūryū* is closely related to the concept of *iki* ("chic"). Both of these qualities are much admired by the Japanese.

It is true of course that a *fūryūjin* is not only a person with a refined sense of beauty; he must also be an educated person of principle. In other words, a *fūryūjin* is a person who has a strong grasp of the basic values and aesthetic sensibilities of the Japanese and who is able to express those values in an elegant and refined way.

□ 中秋の名月 Harvest moon
□ ひんやりとした parky
□ 愛でる to admire
□ 体得する to understand through experience

□ さりげなく casually
□ 心地よく pleasantly
□ 感性 quality

Beauty | *207*

Furigana JAPAN

日本人のこころ

Heart & Soul of the Japanese

2017年11月3日　第1刷発行

著　者　山久瀬洋二

発行者　浦　晋亮

発行所　IBCパブリッシング株式会社
〒162-0804 東京都新宿区中里町29番3号　菱 秀 神楽坂ビル 9F
Tel. 03-3513-4511　Fax. 03-3513-4512
www.ibcpub.co.jp

印刷所　中央精版印刷株式会社

© 2011 Yoji Yamakuse
© 2017 IBC Publishing, Inc.

Printed in Japan

落丁本・乱丁本は、小社宛にお送りください。送料 小社負担にてお取り替えいたします。
本書の無断複写（コピー）は著作権法上での例外を除き禁じられています。

ISBN978-4-7946-0511-5